C I T Y P A C K

Seattle

By Suzanne Tedesko

Fodor's

Fodor's Travel Publications, Inc.
New York • Toronto • London • Sydney • Auckland

WWW.FODORS.COM

Contents

About this book

ORGANIZATION

Citypack Seattle's six sections cover the six most important aspects of your visit to Seattle:

- Seattle life—the city and its people
- Itineraries, a walk, a bicycle ride and excursions—how to organize your time
- The top 25 sights—plotted from west to east
- Different aspects of the city that make it special
- Detailed listings of restaurants, hotels, shops and nightlife
- Practical information

In addition, text boxes provide fascinating extra facts and snippets, highlights of places to visit and invaluable practical advice.

CROSS-REFERENCES

To help you make the most of your visit, cross-references, indicated by ➤ , show you where to find additional information about a place or subject.

MAPS

- **The fold-out map** in the wallet at the back of the book is a comprehensive street plan of Seattle. All map references are to this map. For example, the Space Needle, ➕ **D3** indicates the grid square of the map in which the Space Needle will be found.
- **The city-center maps** on the inside front and back covers are for quick reference. They show the Top 25 Sights, described on pages 24–48, which are clearly plotted by number (**1** – **25**, not page number) from west to east.

PRICES

Where appropriate, an indication of the cost of an establishment is given by **$** signs: **$$$** denotes higher prices, **$$** denotes average prices, while **$** denotes lower charges.

SEATTLE
life

5

INTRODUCING SEATTLE

Seattle is all about mountains and Microsoft, the stunning scenery and the "Seattle sound," cartoons and coffee. Then there's water—everywhere you look—in freshwater lakes, canals, Puget Sound, and the ubiquitous drizzle that optimists like to call "liquid sunshine."

The character of Seattle has been shaped by its comparative youth, by its maritime climate, and above all, by the beauty of its natural surroundings. Outdoor enthusiasts flock to the region's lush forests, mountains, and waterways, and give the city its outdoorsy feel. Wilderness is nearby. The Cascade Mountains rise to the east, dominated by snowcapped volcanoes: Mt. Baker, Glacier Peak, and grandest of all, 14,410-foot Mt. Rainier. To the west lie the rugged Olympic Mountains.

If the flavor of Seattle is the mocha of its excellent cafés, its colors are gray and green. As if unable to make up its mind, the city can be dark and gloomy in the morning and sparkling by afternoon. Or vice versa. And when Seattle sparkles, as it normally does in the summer, life doesn't get much better. With the first indication of spring, residents get giddy: frisbees are resurrected and sunglasses unearthed as people head to the park or putter in their gardens. Trees, parks, and gardens are all around you, and when they're at their best, you'll know why Seattle is called Emerald City.

Seattle's character is both pedestrian and cutting-edge. On the one hand, the Muzak company—purveyor of canned elevator music—has its world headquarters here. On the other, biotechnology companies such as Immunez are exploring new frontiers. The region has produced a number of firsts, from airplanes to outdoor adventure, microcomputers to medicine and music. At one time, references to Seattle as a company town referred to the pre-eminent position of Boeing. Today, Seattle's work culture is

A century of weather jokes

The city's weather, especially its propensity to rain, has been the butt of jokes for who knows how long.

● "Seattle is a moisturing pad disguised as a city."

— Jerry Seinfeld

probably shaped more by software giant Microsoft, located, along with other computer companies, on the burgeoning Eastside.

The city has also become a major player in medical research and education. The Fred Hutchinson Cancer Research Center performs more bone marrow transplants than any other facility in the country, while the University of Washington's School of Medicine receives major research grants and its family practice training is rated tops in the nation. In addition, the excellence of the city's emergency medical services has earned Seattle the dubious distinction of being the best place in America to have a heart attack.

Seattle is short on glitz and big on all things natural. For example, clothing manufacturers with headquarters here produce sportswear of down, Goretex, and fleece, reflecting the area's obsession with the outdoors. Paris it's not, although more and more local designers are creating their own versions of wearable art. And though outdoorsy, Seattle is anything but a cultural wasteland. Outside of New York, the city has the greatest number of professional theater companies in the United States. Cultural life is thriving, with the likes of the Seattle Symphony Orchestra, the Pacific Northwest Ballet, and the Seattle Opera, the only company in the United States to launch Wagner's entire *Ring of the Nibelung* cycle on a regular basis.

The residents of Seattle have developed informality to a high art. Pomposity is anathema and irreverence commonplace. Satirical cartoonist Gary Larson, whose Far Side cartoons debunk human pretension to the very max, is a hometown hero. And if Nirvana and the grunge music scene emerged in the nineties as an angst-ridden reaction to the city's no-worries cultural ethic, Seattle's laid-back climate of tolerance nevertheless enabled grunge to flourish.

The invisible throng

A famous speech by Chief Sealth reminds us of the Seattle area's original inhabitants: "And when the last Red Man shall have perished...these shores will swarm with the invisible dead of my tribe, and when your children's children think themselves alone in the field, the store, the shop, upon the highway, or in the silence of the pathless woods, they will not be alone...At night when the streets of your cities and villages are silent and you think them deserted, they will throng with the returning hosts that once filled them and still love this beautiful land. The White Man will never be alone."

Left: Espresso coffee fuels Seattle's vigorous urban life. The calorie-conscious can order a 'skinny' latte—an espresso with steamed, non-fat milk
Above: The Seattle Times masthead

7

Seattle's population today represents a diverse cultural mix. Roughly 15 percent of residents reportedly speak a language other than English at home, and Seattle's Asian and Pacific Island population has increased by 56 percent in a decade. Asian influence is felt in a Northwest esthetic reminiscent of Japan; in city gardens, fountains, and architecture; and in the sizeable number of Asian restaurants and markets. Sad to say, Seattle's population also includes a large number of homeless—attributable in part to a mild winter climate that attracts people from colder neighboring regions.

As for the weather, most Seattleites take it in their stride. Except for a few transplanted Californians, Seattle residents hardly seem to notice the drizzle and rarely let it slow them down. True natives secretly scoff at those who take shelter under umbrellas or closet themselves indoors at the first hint of rain.

In other ways, Seattle's people are cautious and compliant. They generally mind their manners and avoid making a spectacle of themselves. Clothing is understated, and on the roads, motorists are downright polite. To the exasperation of harried East Coast transplants, Seattle drivers seldom honk. There are, of course, exceptions. Road rage, for instance, is on the rise. And ghoulish teens dressed in black make a statement with irradiated green hair and multiple body piercings that is anything but subtle. At the other end of the spectrum—among the young and affluent—stylish dressing is staging a comeback, along with the Martini.

Not surprisingly, in a city so blessed by its natural surroundings, environmental consciousness is high. Seattle has won kudos for its recycling program and the city is easy for vegetarians. It's tough for smokers, though, as all public buildings and many workplaces and restaurants ban smoking. If you do smoke, your best options at mealtime are taverns and pubs, and Seattle has some good ones.

So, pack your opera glasses and hiking boots, throw away that umbrella, and prepare to do Seattle like a native.

One of the imposing totem poles that decorate Pioneer Square

Bill Gates

Seattle's best-known man is also currently the world's richest. Born in 1956, Bill Gates grew up in Seattle and attended the city's most prestigious private school. During high school, Gates met fellow student Paul Allen. They went on to found Microsoft, the world's most successful software company, which still has its world headquarters in suburban Seattle.

8

SEATTLE IN FIGURES

POPULATION
- Seattle: 516,259 (aged 18 and older 431,329; with college degrees 37.9 percent)
- Metropolitan area including Everett, Tacoma and Bremerton: 2.6 million
- Historic growth: 1878 2,000; 1890 42,000; 1910 237,194; 1930 365,583; 1950 467,591; 1970 530,831

THE CITY
- Latitude: 47°36'32"N
- Longitude: 122°20'12"W
- Depth of Elliott Bay: 150–900 feet
- Number of hills: 12; highest point: West Seattle (512 feet)
- Total square miles: 91.6 (88.5 land; 3.1 water)
- Parks: more than 300, totalling 5,000 acres
- Housing units: 249,032
- Area health clubs: 80
- Rainfall: 34–37 inches per year
- Number of clear days: 56 per year

FIRSTS
- Gas station (1907)
- Public golf course in the United States (1915)
- General strike in the United States (1919)
- Circumnavigational flight from Sandpoint Naval Station (1924)
- Woman mayor (Bertha Landes; 1924)
- Water skis (1928)
- Concrete "floating" bridge (1939)
- Full-scale monorail (1962)
- Covered shopping mall (1950)

The REI store

A CHRONOLOGY

1792 British Captain George Vancouver and his lieutenant, Peter Puget, explore the "inland sea," which Vancouver names Puget Sound.

1851 David Denny, John Low, and Lee Terry reach Alki Point and dub their colony "New York–Alki."

1852 Pioneers move the settlement across Elliott Bay to what is now Pioneer Square.

1853 Henry Yesler begins operating a steam sawmill, establishing the timber industry. President Fillmore signs an act creating the Washington Territory. (Achieves statehood 1889.)

1855 The Port Elliott Treaty, signed by Governor Isaac Stevens, Chief Sealth, and others, banishes Native Americans to reservations.

1856 "The Indian War": American battle sloop *Decatur* fires into downtown to root out native peoples, who burn the settlement.

1861 The University of Washington is established.

1864 Asa Mercer returns from New England with 11 young women (the Mercer Girls) as wives for lonely Seattle bachelors.

1869 The city is incorporated and passes its first public ordinance—a law against drunkenness.

1886 Anti-Chinese riots erupt.

1889 The Great Seattle Fire caused damage exceeding $10 million.

1893 James Hill's Great Northern Railroad reaches its western terminus, Seattle.

1897 The ship *Portland* steams into Seattle carrying "a ton of gold" and triggers the Klondike Gold Rush. Seattle becomes the primary outfitting center for prospectors.

1903	The Seattle Symphony Orchestra is formed.
1907	Pike Place Public Market opens.
1909	Seattle launches its first World's Fair, the Alaska-Yukon-Pacific Exposition.
1909–17	Lake Washington Ship Canal is built.
1914	The 42-story Smith Tower is completed.
1919	The Seattle General Strike: 60,000 workers walk off the job.
1926	Bertha Landes is elected mayor, the first woman mayor of a major American city.
1940	The Lake Washington Floating Bridge links Seattle with Eastside communities.
1941	U.S. entry into World War II. Workers flood into Seattle to work in the shipyards, at Boeing, and elsewhere. The population soars.
1949	An earthquake measuring 7.2 on the Richter scale rocks the area.
1962	Seattle hosts the Century 21 World's Fair.
1963	A second floating bridge, the 1.4-mile Evergreen Point Bridge, is completed.
1970	Boeing lays off 655,000 workers over a two-year period, precipitating a recession.
1971	Starbucks opens in Pike Place Market, launching the nation's specialty coffee craze.
1975	William Gates and Paul Allen start Microsoft.
1980	Mt. St. Helens erupts, showering ash over Seattle, 100 miles away.
1992–4	The success of rock group Nirvana makes Seattle the grunge music capital of the world.

PEOPLE & EVENTS FROM HISTORY

A bust of Chief Sealth in Pioneer Square

Beyond sign language

Early explorers, traders, and Native Americans communicated in Chinook, a language that developed as a trade medium. Seattle pioneers mastered Chinook, and it served as the common language with local tribes. Here are a few everyday terms:

tillicum = friend

illahee = land

klootchman = woman

potlatch = gift

muck-a-muck = food

chickamin = money

chee chacko = newcomer

mashie! = thank you

CHIEF SEALTH

Sealth was born in 1786 on Blake Island. In 1792, the young boy watched "the great canoe with giant white wings"—Captain Vancouver's three-masted brig—sail into Puget Sound. In his 20s, he became leader of the Suquamish, Duwamish, and allied bands, and became a friend to white settlers—so much so that pioneer Arthur Denny suggested changing the settlement's name from "Alki" to "Sealth." Since the name was difficult for whites to pronounce properly, it became corrupted to "Seattle."

THE BIRTH OF TRADE

In December 1852, the brig *Leonesa* sailed into Seattle hoping to find timber for rebuilding parts of San Francisco destroyed by fire. The pioneers had none, but in the next few days, they worked feverishly, cutting trees and hauling them to the waterfront. At this moment, a realization was born: the great forests of the Northwest, hitherto viewed as obstacles to growth, were now seen as a valuable and plentiful resource. Seattle's tie to both timber and trade was assured. The following year, Henry Yesler began operation of the first steam sawmill, firmly establishing the importance of lumber in the region's economy.

THE PORT ELLIOTT TREATY

Preceeding the Indian War of 1856, Territorial Governor Isaac Stevens drafted a settlement and persuaded Chief Sealth and other Native American leaders to sign. The Port Elliott Treaty promised the tribes payments, services, and reservation lands. Fearing that his people would be absorbed by the growing numbers of settlers, Sealth reluctantly signed. In a speech, Chief Sealth imagined his people "ebbing away like a rapidly receding tide that will never return." He implored the whites to "be just and deal kindly with my people, for the dead are not powerless."

SEATTLE
how to organize your time

ITINERARIES

These itineraries can be done on foot or by public transportation. In good
weather take a day trip out of the city (Excursions ➤ 20).

ITINERARY ONE	**DOWNTOWN**
Morning	Starting at the northwest corner of Pike Place Market (➤ 33), meander through the market, stopping at the stalls and shops. Work your way south to 1st and Union, then cross the street to the Seattle Art Museum (➤ 36).
Lunch	Eat at the market, the museum café, or across 1st by the Harbor Steps (➤ 54).
Afternoon	Catch bus 174 southbound on 2nd to the world-class Museum of Flight (➤ 43). Return the same way, but get off close to Pioneer Square (➤ 39), at 4th and Jackson.
Evening	Enjoy an Italian dinner in Pioneer Square or go to nearby Shanghai Garden in the International District (➤ 41). For entertainment, consider a ballgame (➤ 83), music clubs (➤ 80–81), or stand-up comedy (➤ 83) in the area.
ITINERARY TWO	**SEATTLE CENTER TO FREMONT**
Morning	Ride the monorail to Seattle Center (➤ 35). In clear weather, go up the Space Needle for a view (➤ 30), then visit the Pacific Science Center (➤ 29), and catch the IMAX movie (➤ 60).
Lunch	For something simple and fast, eat at the Seattle Center outdoor café or in the Center House foodcourt. If the weather's good, have a picnic by the fountain. For a more formal lunch, try neighborhood restaurants.
Afternoon	Stroll the Center House grounds. For an interactive musical experience, check out the Experience Music Project (➤ 31) before catching bus 82 (1st and Denny) to the offbeat neighborhood of Fremont (➤ 55).

ITINERARY THREE	LAKE UNION TO THE UNIVERSITY
Morning	At the Westlake Center, catch bus 70, 71, 72, or 73 to Lake Union (➤ 37). Exit on the S/SE side and look around the area between Yale Landing and Chandler's Cove. Rent a small boat and go out on the water or else take a guided tour.
Lunch	Try one of the restaurants on the eastern shore.
Afternoon	Catch bus 70, 71, 72, or 73 to the University of Washington (➤ 44), and visit the Burke Museum (➤ 46). Then relax in the café or in the fossil courtyard before walking to Red Square and going to the Henry Gallery (➤ 45). Leave the campus via Rainier Vista, noting the great view, and catch the 25 bus along Montlake Boulevard. If time and energy permit, stop en route at the REI outdoor store (➤ 40). Afterwards, with your bus transfer slip, re-board the 25 for downtown.
ITINERARY FOUR	WATERFRONT TO BAINBRIDGE ISLAND
Morning	From Pike Place Market (➤ 33), walk down the Hillclimb to the Seattle Aquarium (➤ 32), then continue south to catch the ferry to Bainbridge Island (➤ 34). Walk the half-mile into town and stick your head into the shops along Winslow Way.
Lunch	Eat in town at Café Nola (➤ 69) or buy something from a deli.
Afternoon	Visit Bainbridge Island Winery to sample local wines. If you have a car, drive to Bloedel Reserve for an afternoon walk (reservations required) or cross Agate Pass to Suquamish Museum.
Evening	Drop in at the Harbour Public House (➤ 82), where the locals go for fish and chips, then ride the ferry back as the sun sets.

15

WALKS

THE SIGHTS

- Freeway Park (➤ 50)
- Rainier Square
- Blueprints: 100 Years of Seattle Architecture – free exhibit by the Museum of History and Industry (➤ 58)
- Fifth Avenue Theater (➤ 54)
- City Center (➤ 35)
- Westlake Center
- Westlake Park
- Pike Place Market (➤ 33)

Freeway Park's waterfall

INFORMATION

Distance 1–1½ miles
Start point The Washington Convention Center, 8th and Pike

➕ E6

🚌 7, 10, 43 on Pike

End point Harbor Steps, University St. Between 1st Ave. & Western

➕ F6

🚌 Waterfront streetcar

CITY CENTER TO PIKE PLACE MARKET

Begin at the Seattle/King County Visitor Center on the galleria level of the Washington State Convention and Trade Center. Pick up a calender of events and a discount coupon book; then walk to the central lobby, where you'll pass under an imposing carved Native doorway ("Kwakiutl" tribe) to board the escalator to level 4. Exit through Freeway Park to the park's southwest corner. Descend the concrete stairs through the Canyon waterfall, designed to mask traffic noise from the freeway underneath. Leave the park at 6th and University, cross University, and climb the stairs to Union Square for a view of the city from the spacious plaza. Now double back to University, heading west to Rainier Square. Peruse the Seattle architecture exhibit—level 3—and exit on 5th across from the Fifth Avenue Theater (➤ 54) and Eddie Bauer (➤ 70). Head north across Union, past the City Center, and cross Pike and Pine to the Westlake Center.

Coffee break Look left for the glass-walled Seattle's Best Coffee, opposite Westlake Park, a good place to stop for a coffee.

The market Head down Pine to 1st. Walk north one block to Stewart, go left for half a block to Post Alley, and right down the narrow way to Virginia. Stroll past Pike Place Fish, where the clerks and countermen hurl salmon through the air. Continue south until you are facing Tenzing Momo Herbal Apothecary; then head down the stairs on your left, winding along an interior corridor past Pike Place Brewery until you come out at 1st and Union across from Seattle Art Museum. One block south, at 1st Avenue and University, you'll reach Harbor Steps (➤ 54).

WATERFRONT TO PIONEER SQUARE

Stroll down the Harbor Steps and amble south along the Waterfront to Yesler. Turn left and walk to the corner of 1st and Yesler, site of Pioneer Square's pergola. Smith Tower is one block east. Cross to the east side of 1st and walk south, taking time to drift into shops along the way. Cross Washington, pass Grand Central Arcade, and continue across Main to the Elliott Bay Bookstore Café. Stop for a coffee or to browse the bookshelves, then proceed along 1st to Jackson and go left one block to cobblestoned Occidental, then left again onto its pedestrian mall. Step into the shops and galleries along the way, and if possible, catch a glass-blowing demonstration at Glasshouse Art Glass.

After the goldrush At Main, visit the Klondike Gold Rush National Historic Park, just left of Occidental. The museum commemorates Seattle's role as an outfitting center for prospectors. As you exit, turn right and walk past Occidental Park, noting the totem poles, to Waterfall Park, a serene oasis at 2nd Avenue. Walk right on 2nd one block to Jackson, then turn left. Proceed two blocks east past the giant Kingdome. Continue past King Street Railroad Station and Union Station to the Metro Bus Tunnel International District station. Catch a northbound bus and get off at University station. (You can also take a bus on 2nd Avenue.

Falcons on TV Now, walk to Washington Mutual's blue tower (▶ 54) at 3rd and Seneca, where a video camera poised on the rooftop records the activities of two peregrine falcons that return each year to nest. Inside the lobby, you can watch the birds live on a monitor. End your tour by walking uphill one block to the elegant Four Seasons Olympic Hotel, where you can relax and enjoy a drink in the Garden Court or sample local oysters at Shuckers.

THE SIGHTS

- Waterfront (▶ 32)
- Pioneer Square (▶ 39)
- Smith Tower (▶ 54)
- Glasshouse Art Glass (▶ 58)
- Klondike Gold Rush National Historic Park
- Occidental Park totems (▶ 53)
- Waterfall Park
- Kingdome
- Washington Mutual Building (▶ 54)

INFORMATION

Distance 1–1½ miles
Start point Harbor Steps, 1st and University
🔖 F6
🚎 Waterfront Streetcar
End point Four Seasons Olympic Hotel, 4th and University
🔖 F6
🚌 Free bus zone

Pioneer Square street scene

EVENING STROLLS

Join the locals for an evening stroll around Green Lake Park

GREEN LAKE

An evening stroll around Green Lake is a great way to watch Seattleites doing what they like most—relaxing outdoors. On fine days, you'll see a whole cross-section of energetic types, including bikers, joggers, speed-walkers, dog-walkers, skaters, and frisbee-players. The paved 2.8-mile loop that encircles the lake has two lanes—one for pedestrians, the other for people on wheels—and a variety of lovely old trees provide shade along the way.

Everyone from toddlers to seniors training for one last marathon converge on the Green Lake trail, and ducks and Canada geese compete with humans for sovereignty of the coveted grassy areas. Along the trail, you'll pass the intimate Bathhouse Theater (➤ 78), two swimming beaches, a golf course, fishing piers, boat rentals, tennis courts, and a community center and pool.

ELLIOTT BAY TRAIL

This 2.5 mile walking and biking trail begins on the north end of the pier 70 parking lot at Myrtle Edwards Park and winds along the water through Elliott Bay Park. Soon, the divided path swings around three huge granite slabs, which together make up Michael Heizer's controversial sculpture *Adjacent, Against, Upon.* Continuing north, you'll pass the enormous grain terminal and loading dock where wheat and other grain from eastern Washington and the Midwest, brought in by rail, is loaded onto ships bound for foreign ports. The trail continues through Elliott Bay Park and terminates just past a public fishing dock.

INFORMATION

Green Lake
Distance About 3 miles
Start and end point car park, Greenlake Community Center (East Greenlake Drive)
🚻 K2, L2
🚌 Bus: 16, 26

Myrtle Edwards/Elliott Bay Park
Distance 2½ miles
Start and end point Pier 70 at Broad Street and Alaskan Way, north end of parking lot
🚻 D2
🚌 Bus 1 or 2 to 1st and W Bay, or waterfront trolley

ORGANIZED SIGHTSEEING

ON THE WATER

Argosy Tours (☎ 206 623–4252). One-hour harbor cruises; 2½-hour tours through the lakes and Hiram M Chittenden Locks (pier 57) and the "Sleepless in Seattle" Lake Union/ Lake Washington loop. Over the holidays, Argosy operates "Christmas Ship" cruises. Pier 55–56 for harbor cruises; lake cruises from 1200 Westlake .

Discover Houseboating (☎ 206/322–9157). Tours on Lake Union, tailored to your interests. (Walking tours as well).

Spirit of Puget Sound (☎ 206/674–3500). Lunch, dinner, and moonlight cruises on Elliott Bay. Buffet, shows, and dance bands. Daily from pier 70.

Sport Fishing of Seattle (☎ 206/623–6364 for reservations). Tours depart pier 54 for a day of salmon and bottom fishing on Puget Sound. Daily.

ON LAND

Gray Line Tours (☎ 206/626–5208 or 800/426–7505). City bus tours; "Grapes and Hops" to winery and brewery; Boeing tours; day and overnight trips to Mt. Rainier, Vancouver, Victoria, B.C., the Olympic Peninsula, and the San Juan Islands.

Kingdome Tours (☎ 206/296–3128). Behind-the-scenes walking tour of the facility and sports museum.

Seattle Tours (☎ 206/660–8687). Small group tours in vans; downtown pickup.

Scenic Bound Tours Co. (☎ 206/433–6907; FAX 206/246–5505). Day trips to Mt. Rainier National Park, June 20–Oct. 31, including walks and hikes in the Northwest wilderness. Also available to Mt. St. Helens and the Olympic Peninsula.

Viewpoints Architectural Walking Tours (☎ Tour Hotline: 206/667–9186). Walking tours to a variety of downtown and residential sites, May–Nov.

FROM THE AIR

Seattle Seaplanes (☎ 206/329–9638 or 1–800/637–5553). Flights over Seattle and environs. Daily departures from east shore of Lake Union.

Bi-plane Tours (☎ 206/763–9706). In open-cockpit restored planes, Apr–Oct. Galvin Flying Service.

Tillicum Village/Blake Island

This four-hour excursion to Blake Island, which includes a narrated harbor tour, salmon dinner, and stunning theatrical presentation of Native American legend, touches on nearly every highlight of the Northwest: you'll see views, and lush vegetation, and get a chance to ply the waters, hike forest trails, experience Native American culture, and sample quality entertainment. Year-round from pier 56. ☎ 206/443–1244.

EXCURSIONS

INFORMATION

Mt. Rainier
Distance 70 miles southeast of
Seattle
Journey time 3 hours by road.
Route I-5 south to Tacoma; east on
512; south on route 7 and
east on route 706 to the park
entrance
Bus tours Gray Line
(☎ 206/624–5813 or
800/426–7532) or
Scenic Bound Tours
(☎ 206/433–6907)
Mt. Rainier National Park
(☎ 360/569–2211)
Paradise Visitor Center
(☎ 360/589–2275)

Victoria, British Columbia
Journey time 2–3 hours, one-way
☎ For *Victoria Clipper*
206/448–5000

*The Empress Hotel
dominates Victoria's
pretty harborfront*

The excursions in this section are most easily done by car. The Hurricane Ridge and Whidbey Island trips require ferry rides; keep in mind that delays can be considerable at the terminals, especially in summer and on weekends.

MT. RAINIER

Known simply as "the mountain," Mt. Rainier is the jewel in the crown of Washington's peaks. It rises 14,410 feet above sea level, and the upper 6,000 to 7,000 feet are covered in snow and ice year-round. On clear Seattle days, its white dome hovers over the city with an awesome presence so immediate, it's hard to believe it's 70 miles away. Small wonder that native peoples ascribed supernatural power to this active volcano, one of a string running south from the Canadian border to California. Since there's no public transportation to Mt. Rainier, plan to drive and explore on your own, or take one of the bus tour. For information on hiking, stop at Longmire, then drive 11 miles to the Paradise Visitor Center, the take-off point for various hikes. (The center is open daily but hours vary seasonally.)

VICTORIA, BRITISH COLUMBIA

Cruise northern Puget Sound and the Strait of Juan de Fuca aboard the *Victoria Clipper*, a high-speed catamaran, and sail directly into Victoria's beautiful Inner Harbor. Be prepared for company, though, as tourists pour into this provincial capital for a taste of merry England, and Victoria obliges with formal gardens, double-decker buses, and shops selling tweeds and Irish linen. If that's not your cup of tea, it's still a lovely trip, especially with a window seat on the *Clipper's* upper deck. See the excellent Northwest Coast artifacts at the Royal British Columbia Museum and, if you choose, meander through the ever-popular Butchart Gardens or indulge yourself with tea in the imperial splendour of the Empress Hotel. Multiple daily roundtrips provide visitors some flexibility in determining how long to stay in Victoria.

HURRICANE RIDGE/OLYMPIC NATIONAL PARK

Take the ferry to Bainbridge Island (➤ 34). From there, take 305 west to 3 north, then pick up 104. Follow 20 to Port Townsend, pausing for coffee or lunch in this Victorian town before doubling back to 101 west and Port Angeles. Turn south on Hurricane Ridge Road and drive the 17 winding miles to the Olympic National Park Visitor Center. Walk the 1½-mile trail to Hurricane Hill, watching for marmot and deer. To see the Elwha River rainforest, return to Port Angeles, continuing west on 101 the short distance to Olympic Hot Springs Road. Feast your eyes on the lush vegetation and watch for elk. From here, retrace the route to Seattle, stopping at Sequim if you have energy and time, to walk Dungeness Spit, or drive through Olympic Game Farm. Stop at Three Crabs for cracked crab, and call it a day.

INFORMATION

Hurricane Ridge/Olympic National Park
Distance 190 mile round trip
Journey time: 2½ hours by road to Port Townsend (a long day trip)
Route Ferry to Bainbridge Island, west through Kitsap to the Olympic Peninsula
Olympic National Park Visitor Center 360/452–0330

WHIDBEY ISLAND/LA CONNER

Drive past Boeing's 747 plant (➤ 48) to Mukilteo. Take the Whidbey ferry, then drive into Langley for exploration, coffee, and goodies. Take 20 north, turning off at Fort Casey to climb the battlements and walk the bluff. Continue to Coupeville for something to eat, and proceed north to dramatic Deception Pass. For a picnic or walk on the beach, follow the signs to state beaches, mostly littered with washed-up logs. Continue on 20, swinging east to the Farmhouse Inn, and turn right onto Best Road. Drive through farmland to the 19th-century town of La Conner. Explore on your own, then stop for refreshments before heading southeast to Conway and I-5 southbound.

INFORMATION

Whidbey Island/La Conner Loop
Distance 160 mile loop
Journey time A long day trip
Route I-5 north to Mukilteo ferry; on Whidbey, route 525 to 20 north
↔ Skagit Valley tulip fields—April is peak season—for information and maps call 800/488–5477

WHAT'S ON

JANUARY   *Chinese and Vietnamese New Year's Celebration*
Martin Luther King Celebration

FEBRUARY   *Fat Tuesday*: a week-long Mardi Gras celebration in Pioneer Square

MARCH   *Imagination Celebration/Art Festival for Kids*
Seattle Fringe Festival

APRIL   *Cherry Blossom and Japanese Cultural Festival*

MAY   *Opening Day of Yachting Season* (first Saturday): races on Lakes Union and Washington
International Children's Theater Festival: first-rate performances by groups from around the world
University Street Fair: crafts and entertainment
Northwest Folklife Festival: the largest folk festival in the country
Pike Place Market Festival: food, music, crafts
Seattle International Film Festival

JUNE   *Fremont Solstice Parade and Celebration*: elaborate costumes and floats to celebrate 21 June, longest day of the year
Fremont Arts and Crafts Fair: crafts, food
Out to Lunch Summer Downtown Concerts
Summer Nights on the Pier Concert Series

JULY   *Fourth of July*: fireworks over Lake Union and Elliott Bay
Lake Union Wooden Boat Festival
Caribbean Festival–A Taste of Soul: food, music
Chinatown International District Summer Festival: performances, food, crafts
Bite of Seattle Food Fest
Pacific Northwest Arts and Crafts Fair
Seafair: everything from milk-carton derbies and hydrofoil heats to Indian pow-wows

SEPTEMBER   *Bumbershoot*: festival of music, visual arts, crafts

OCTOBER   *Northwest Bookfest*: literary festival

DECEMBER   *Christmas Ship*: brightly lit vessels make the rounds of the beaches with vocal groups aboard who sing carols to people along the shore

SEATTLE's
top 25 sights

The sights are shown on the maps on the inside front cover and inside back cover, numbered **1–25** *from west to east across the city*

1

DISCOVERY PARK

Discovery Park is the largest stand of wilderness in the city. Its meadows, marshes, forests, cliffs, and shoreline provide habitat for many birds and animals, including fox and coyote.

Legacy of the military The 520 forested acres on Magnolia Bluff that is today's Discovery Park was a military base from the 1890s, but in 1970, the government turned it over to the city for use as a park. During the transfer, an alliance of local tribes decided to take the opportunity to regain ancestral land they felt was theirs, and eventually, 19 acres were set aside for a Native American cultural center.

Discover the trails The park's great size means that there are miles of nature, fitness, and bike trails to be explored. To the west, 2 miles of beach extend north and south from the West Point lighthouse (head south for sand, north for rocks). To get to the beach, pick up the loop trail at the north or south parking lot. The park's Visitor Center provides free 90-minute walks led by a naturalist, every Saturday at 2PM.

Daybreak Star Art Center The structure uses enormous cedar timbers to reflect the points of a star. Native art adorns the walls inside. The Center's Sacred Circle Gallery of American Indian Art is one of only four showcases dedicated to contemporary Native American work in the country.

Detail of one of the artworks inside Daybreak Star

ALKI BEACH

Alki's tawny strand and beachfront eateries are as close as Seattle gets to Southern California.

Beginnings The Duwamish and Suquamish peoples were on hand to meet the schooner *Exact* when it sailed into Elliott Bay on 13 November 1851. The ship anchored off Alki Point and Arthur Denny and his party of 23 paddled their skiff ashore. The locals proved friendly and the Denny party decided to stay. They set about building four log cabins, wistfully naming their new home New York–Alki, "Alki" being a word in the Chinook language for "someday," an indication of Denny's ambitions. The following year, after surviving fierce winter storms, the settlers decided to move across Elliott Bay to the more sheltered, deepwater harbor that is today's Pioneer Square.

Beach life The beach itself is the main attraction today. There are great views, fine sand, a paved trail, and boat and bike rentals. There's food and drink, too—try Pegasus (for pizza) and the Alki Bakery (for cookies and other sweets). You can walk, bike, or skate the 2½ miles from Alki Beach to Duwamish Head. If you wish, continue south along the water to lovely Lincoln Park where an outdoor saltwater pool and waterslide invite a refreshing dip (▶ 51).

INFORMATION

- L2
- 3201 Alki Avenue SW (Alki Point Light Station)
- 206/217–6123
- Lighthouse tours Sat/Sun afternoons, May–Aug
- 37 from 2nd Avenue
- Wheelchair access along paved trail
- Lincoln Park (▶ 51)
- Bike, inline skate, and boat rentals (▶ 56–57); driftwood fires permitted on beach

The Alki Point Light Station looks across Puget Sound

3

THE HIRAM M. CHITTENDEN LOCKS

DID YOU KNOW?

- When they were dedicated on 4 July 1917, the Ballard Locks were the second largest in the world
- The locks enable vessels to be raised or lowered between 6 and 26 feet, as necessitated by the tides and lake level
- The average passage through the large lock takes 25 minutes, 10 minutes through the small one; large ocean-going vessels require a half an hour

INFORMATION

- ✚ L2
- ✉ 3015 NW 54th Street
- ☎ 206/783–7059
- ◐ Locks and gardens: daily, 7AM–9PM; Visitor Center: Daily Jun–Sept, 10–7; Oct–May, Thu–Mon 11–5. Closed Thaksgiving, Christmas, and New Year's Day
- ▣ 17 from 4th Avenue
- ♿ Very good
- 🅵 Free
- ↔ Golden Gardens Beach Park (➤ 50), Nordic Heritage Museum (➤ 52)
- ❓ Best months for fish ladder viewing: July and Aug

Above: The turbulent waters of the Chittenden Locks

Legions of boat-owners pass through these locks when taking their boats from lake moorings into Puget Sound. It's interesting to see the boats but equally fascinating is watching the salmon climb the fish ladder through the underwater viewing window.

A dream comes true The 1917 opening of the Ballard Locks and Lake Washington Ship Canal was the fulfillment of a 60-year-old pioneer dream to build a channel that would link Lake Washington and Puget Sound. Primitive construction attempts were made in the 1880s, but it wasn't until Major Hiram M. Chittenden, regional director of the Army Corps of Engineers, won Congressional approval in 1910, that work begin in earnest. Over the next six years, workers excavated and moved thousands of tons of earth with giant steam shovels. The locks are operated from a control tower that regulates the spillway gates and flashes directions to boats. Displays in the nearby visitor center explain the history and construction of the locks and ship canal. One-hour guided tours leave from the center on weekends at 2PM.

Watch the fish A fish ladder, built into the locks, allows salmon and steelhead to move upstream from the sea to their spawning grounds. By sensing "attraction water" at the fish ladder's entrance, the fish find the narrow channel and begin the long journey to the very freshwater spot where they began life. Here, they lay their eggs and die.

Botanical Gardens Nearby, you can also explore the 7-acre Carl S. English Jr. Botanical Gardens, which are planted with more than 500 species from around the world.

FISHERMEN'S TERMINAL

There's something incredibly compelling about seeing fishing boat crews unloading the catch, mending nets, and readying their boats. Fishermen's Terminal is a great place to soak up the hustle and bustle of a large fishing port.

Early days Fish have been an important local resource since Seattle's early days, when the Shilshloh people from Salmon Bay first shared their bountiful harvest with other local tribes. With white settlement, fishing became an important local industry. In the early 1900s, a growing demand for salmon prompted the industry to lure new fishermen to the area—especially Scandinavian, Greek, and Slavic immigrants—many of whose descendants still work in the fishing trade. In 1913, the Port of Seattle designated Fishermen's Terminal on Salmon Bay as home base for the North Pacific fishing fleet. Today Washington fishers harvest 50 percent of all fish and other seafood caught in the United States.

Fishermen's Memorial Dominating the terminal's central plaza, a 30-foot-high column commemorates those Northwest fishermen who lost their lives at sea. Their names, inscribed at the memorial sculpture's base, remind us that fishing was—and is— extremely dangerous work and that the sea can be cruelly unforgiving.

DID YOU KNOW?

- More than 700 commercial fishing boats are based at the terminal, many bound for Alaska
  - Gillnetters, purse seiners, and trawlers thow nets to trap fish; longliners and trollers use lines
- Trollers have a characteristic midship pole, hung at a 45-degree angle, to which baited lines are secured and trolled through the water

INFORMATION

- ✚ L2
- ✉ 3919 18th Avenue W at Salmon Bay
- ☎ 206/728–3395
- ◷ 24 hours
- 🚌 15 or 18 from 1st Avenue (Exit at south end of Ballard Bridge)
- ♿ Very good
- 🎟 Free
- ↔ Discovery Park (▶ 24)
- ❓ A wild fish market, grocery, gallery, and marine shops

The Fishermen's Memorial is topped by a bronze sculpture of a halibut fisherman

27

5

WOODLAND PARK ZOO

INFORMATION

- ✠ L2
- ✉ 5500 Phinney Avenue N
- ☎ 206/684–4800
- 🕐 Daily, mid-Mar to mid-Oct: 9:30–6; mid-Oct to mid-Mar: 9:30–4
- 🍴 Rain Forest Café, on site
- 🚌 5 (from 6th and Westlake)
- ♿ Wheelchair rentals at south gate
- 💲 Expensive; half-price with purchase of CityPass
- ↔ Green Lake (➤ 47)
- ❓ Special family events; rose garden, summer concerts, Wed nights, July and Aug (Concert Hotline: 206/615-0076). Zoo store

Woodland Park Zoo is recognized as a world leader in showing animals in conditions that emulate their native habitats. The zoo has also won international acclaim for its conservation efforts, including a successful captive breeding program.

Running free (almost) Most animals roam freely in their simulated "bioclimatic zones." Four new exhibits—African Savanna, Tropical Rain Forest, Northern Trail (Alaska), and Elephant Forest—have won prestigious awards and introduced zoo visitors not only to the animals, but also to corresponding plant species and ecosystems. The caged enclosures that remain—in the Family Farm and petting zoo area—invite young children to get up-close-and-personal with lambs, pigs, goats, and other farm animals. The zoo's newest exhibit, Trail of Vines, showcases macaques, tapirs, pythons, and orang-utans in a setting representing the forests of western India and northern Borneo.

Roses and concerts Woodland Park's lovely Rose Garden contains almost 5,000 roses, which bloom between May and August and normally peak during the first week of July. Here, new hybrid varieties of rose are test-grown for one of the country's leading growers. Summer attractions at the zoo include the outdoor concert series, with renowned folk and blues artists.

Gorilla mother and child at Woodland Park Zoo

PACIFIC SCIENCE CENTER

As you enter the Science Center's grounds, you step into another world. Soaring gothic arches and an inner courtyard of reflecting pools, platforms, and footbridges indicate you are in for something special. You won't be disappointed.

Sputnik's legacy In 1962, the American scientific community was still smarting from the Soviet Union's unexpected launch of the Sputnik spacecraft. Determined to restore confidence in American science and technology, U.S. officials pulled out all the stops when they built the U.S. Science Pavilion for the Seattle World's Fair. The building reopened after the fair ended as the Pacific Science Center.

Science made easy A visit to the Pacific Science Center can happily fill half a day. The interactive exhibits bring scientific principles to life and make learning fun. In an outdoor exhibit, Water Works, you can maneuver a water cannon to activate whirligigs or attempt to move a 2-ton ball suspended on water. Nearby, children can ride a high-rail bike for a bird's-eye view of proceedings. The Body Works exhibition lets you measure your stress level, grip strength, and mental concentration, or see what your face looks like with two left sides. In the Tech Zone's Virtual Basketball installation, you stand against a backdrop, put on a virtual reality glove, and by moving an arm, transport yourself to a computer screen where you can go one-on-one against an on-screen opponent. The Science Playground and Brain Game areas use giant levers, spinning rooms, and baseball batting cages to teach the principles of physics. Small children like blowing giant bubbles and climbing the rocket in the Kids' Zone. Next door is the IMAX 3-D Theater.

DID YOU KNOW?

- Designed by: Minoru Yamasaki
- Built as the US Science Pavilion for the 1962 World's Fair
- The first museum in the United States to be founded as a science and technology center

INFORMATION

- ✚ D2
- ✉ 200 Second Avenue N (Seattle Center)
- ☎ 206/443–2001; Website: www.pacsci.org
- 🕐 Summer: Daily, 10–6; Other times: Mon–Fri 10–5; Sat/Sun, holidays: 10–6
- 🍴 Fountains Café on site; daily 10–5
- 🚌 1, 2, 13, 24, 33
- 🚝 Monorail
- ♿ Very good
- 💰 Moderate; half-price with CityPass
- ↔ Monorail (➤ 35), Space Needle (➤ 30), Experience Music Project (➤ 31), Attractions for children (➤ 60)
- ❓ IMAX 3-D theater; Laser Theater presents family matinees and evening rock shows

Above: Hands-on fun at the Water Works exhibit   29

SPACE NEEDLE

INFORMATION

- D3
- Seattle Center
- 206/443-2111 or 800/937-9582
- Daily till midnight
- Emerald Suite, rotating restaurant at the top ($$$)
- 3, 4, 6
- Monorail
- Wheelchair access
- Expensive; half-price with CityPass; free with dinner at restaurant
- Monorail (➤ 35), Pacific Science Center (➤ 29), Experience Music Project (➤ 31), Attractions for children (➤ 60)

The Needle's height and futuristic design have made it Seattle's most recognized landmark. The view from the observation deck is fantastic. If you ride in the glass-walled elevator to the top during a snow-storm, it appears to be snowing upward.

The city's symbol The 605-foot Space Needle was built in 1962 for Seattle's futuristic World's Fair. Rising 200 feet above Seattle's highest hill, the structure is visible over a wide area. The steel structure weighs 3,700 tons and is anchored into the foundation with 72 huge bolts, each 32 feet long by 4 inches in diameter. The structure is designed to withstand winds up to 150mph, although the glass elevators are closed when winds top 60mph.

Observation deck Each year, over a million visitors ride one of the three glass elevators to the observation deck at the 520-foot level. Views from here are stunning when the weather is clear, and informative displays point out more than 60 sites around the area. High-resolution telescopes

let you zoom in on objects for a closer view. A reservation at either of two restaurants on the 500 level gets you to the observation deck without paying. Rotating one complete turn every hour, the Emerald Suite Restaurant lets you take in the full 360-degree panorama in the course of a meal.

A view of Seattle from the Needle's observation deck

EXPERIENCE MUSIC PROJECT

It seems fitting that the city is entering the 21st century with a new rock 'n' roll museum. After all, local 1990s grunge bands like Nirvana put Seattle on the world music map.

Seattle rocks The EMP, opening in fall 1999, came into being to celebrate creativity and innovation as they're expressed through American popular music, primarily by rock 'n' roll. State-of-the-art interactive installations will enable visitors to "get into the act." The project will also showcase Northwest rock & roll memorabilia.

A fan's plan The Experience Music Project is Microsoft co-founder Paul Allen's gift to the city. Allen, who idolized Seattle-born Jimi Hendrix, bankrolled the project and set up a foundation to execute the plan. Sparing no expense, he hired the celebrated architect Frank Gehry to design a suitably outrageous structure. Even before its foundation was laid, critics were calling the building "The Thing," based on photographs of the model. As if the structure itself isn't daring enough, Gehry's radical design called for rerouting the monorail through an upper corner of the building so visitors are able to get a bird's-eye view of the museum below.

DID YOU KNOW?

- Jazz musician Les Paul pioneered electric guitar technology in Seattle by using a solid body. The Gibson company adopted the design and use it to this day
- Jimi Hendrix was born in Seattle in 1942. In the late '60s he revolutionized electric guitar playing a radical fusion of jazz, rock, soul, and blues

INFORMATION

- ➕ D3
- ✉ Fifth Avenue N. between Harrison and Broad
- ☎ Website: www.experience.org
- 3, 4, 6 ↔
- Monorail (➤ 35), Pacific Science Center (➤ 29), Space Needle (➤ 31)

Jimi Hendrix, Seattle native and guitar hero

THE WATERFRONT & AQUARIUM

HIGHLIGHTS

The waterfront
- Bell Street complex restaurants and marina
- Waterfront trolley
- Odyssey Maritime Discovery Center
- Omnidome

The aquarium
- Children's please touch tank
- Underwater dome room
- Coral reef exhibit

INFORMATION

The waterfront
- ✉ Alaskan Way between Broad (pier 70) and Main (pier 48)
- 🚌 Bus 33; Waterfront streetcar

The aquarium
- ✚ F5
- ✉ Pier 59: 1483 Alaskan Way at Pike Street
- ☎ 206/386–4300; recorded message: 206/386–4320
- 🕐 Daily: June–Aug, 10–7; Sept–May, 10–5
- 🍴 Steamers Seafood Cafe on site (► 65)
- 🚋 Waterfront streetcar (Pike Street station)
- ♿ Very good
- 💲 Moderate; half-price with CityPass

Above: The aquarium's underwater dome

The history of Seattle is, in large part, a history of its waterfront. The city's economic and cultural growth has been closely tied to waterfront activity since 1853, when Henry Yesler built the first sawmill there.

Beginnings When pioneers settled along Elliott Bay's eastern shores in 1852, the only flat land suitable for building was a narrow strip along the water, where 1st Avenue runs today. A century later, Seattle's physical landscape had changed dramatically, after a large expanse of Elliott Bay was reclaimed. Maritime industrial activity had moved south to pier 46 and below, and the expanded downtown waterfront was ripe for new beginnings.

Watery hub Import stores, restaurants, excursion boat docks, and curio shops dot the waterfront today. Go for a walk and explore. The Bell Street complex at pier 66 has a conference center, eateries, a marina, and the Odyssey Maritime Discovery Center. Nearby, at pier 69, the port headquarters houses a variety of public art, including an indoor stream that runs the length of the building. You are welcome to stop in. If your taste runs to the bizarre, head for Ye Olde Curiosity Shop, an antiques store, and meet Sylvester the mummy. A picturesque trolley picks up passengers and drops them off along the waterfront, then loops north to Pioneer Square and the International District.

Seattle Aquarium This is *the* place to acquaint yourself with Northwest marine life. Children enjoy handling critters in the touch-tank outdoors; inside, in the underwater dome room you can watch Puget Sound's "underworld" pass before your eyes.

PIKE PLACE MARKET

Pike Place Market is Seattle's heart and soul. Here, people of every background converge, from downtown professionals and Asian farmers to hippie artisans and fascinated tourists.

Farmers' market Pike Place Market was founded in 1907 so that farmers could sell directly to the consumer and eliminate the middleman. It was an immediate success, and grew quickly until World War II precipitated a decline. Threatened by demolition in the 1960s, it's now protected as a Historic District.

Feast for the senses The three-block area stretching between Pike and Virginia has flowerstalls, fishsellers, produce displays, tea shops, bakeries, herbal apothecaries, magic stores, and much more. Street musicians play Peruvian pipes and sing the blues, and the fragrance of flowers and fresh bread fills the air. This is old Seattle frozen in time.

Exploring the market Pick up a map from the information booth (1st Ave. and Pike St, near the big clock) and head out from the sculpture of Rachel the pig. Watch out for the flying fish (at Pike Place Fish), stop to admire the artfully arranged produce and flower displays, and make a sweep around the crafts area, where superb handmade items are sold.

HIGHLIGHTS

Market Arcade
- Shops: Read All About It (for newspapers), DiLaurenti's Grocery and Deli, Market Spice Teas, Tenzing Momo
- Restaurants: Athenian Inn, Sound View Café, Place Pigalle, Maximiliens

Sanitary Market Building/ Post Alley
- Shops: Jack's Fish Spot, Milagros, Made in Washington

Nearby
- Shops: Sur La Table, Seattle Garden Center, Le Panier Bakery, the original Starbucks
- Restaurants: Café Campagne, Chez Shea

INFORMATION

- ✚ F5
- ✉ 1st Avenue between Stewart and Union
- ☎ 206/682–7453
- 🕐 Daily: Mon–Sat 9–6; Sun 11–5; closed on some national holidays
- 🚌 Various along Pike and 1st–4th Avenue (free ride zone). Waterfront streetcar (Pike Street station)
- ♿ Poor
- ↔ Seattle Art Museum (➤ 36), Pioneer Square (➤ 39), Seattle Aquarium (➤ 32)

Pike Place Fish Co. is admired for its range of seafood

11

FERRY TO BAINBRIDGE ISLAND

INFORMATION

Bainbridge Ferry
- E3, G5
- Colman Dock, pier 52; Alaskan Way and Marion
- 206/464–6400
- From Seattle, 6AM–2AM; from Bainbridge, last ferry at 1:15AM
- Buses 16, 66 to ferry. Waterfront streetcar
- Some ferries
- S for walk-on's; SS for car

Bainbridge Island Winery
- 682 Highway 305
- 206/842–9463

Bloedel Reserve
- 7521 NE Dolphin Drive

Suquamish Museum
- 1538 Sandy Hook Road
- 360/598–3311
- Daily 10–5

On a clear day, there's nowhere more delightful than riding the ferry to Bainbridge; standing at the stern to look at the city. The ride is a great way to get views of all that makes Seattle Seattle.

The ferry It takes just 35 minutes to get to Bainbridge Island from the downtown waterfront. En route, you'll see an amazing panorama: the Seattle cityscape, Mt. Rainier to the east, and Bainbridge Island and the snow-capped Olympic Range to the west.

Touring on foot Once you disembark at the Bainbridge ferry dock, walk the short distance to the town of Winslow, visit the charming boutiques, browse at Eagle Harbor Books, stop for lunch at Café Nola (▶ 69), or order treats from the Bainbridge Bakery. If it's Saturday, catch the market on the Winslow green, or, Wednesday to Sunday, visit Bainbridge's Island Winery for tours and tasting. If you're synchronizing your return with the sunset, you could linger at the Harbour Public House (▶ 82).

Touring by car or bike If you have wheels, you can visit Bloedel Reserve and walk exquisite trails (you'll need to have called in advance for reservations). Continuing across Agate Pass Bridge, you will enter Port Madison Indian Reservation and the town of Suquamish, where Chief Sealth is buried. Suquamish Museum recounts the cultural history of this tribe.

The city drops away as the ferry heads to Bainbridge

12

MONORAIL TO SEATTLE CENTER

Riding the Monorail to Seattle Center is like being in an old sci-fi movie. You buzz the city like some giant insect, sweeping past the Space Needle before alighting outside the Center House.

World's Fair leftovers The Seattle Center district, like the monorail, is the legacy of the 1962 World's Fair. Once a Native American ceremonial ground, and later host to traveling circuses, the 74-acre site didn't assume its present form until the fair. The monorail has now run continuously longer than any other monorail in the world.

Museum city Every day, this elevated train carries up to 7,000 passengers between Westlake Center, Seattle's retail core, and Seattle Center, its entertainment hub. There, you can go on amusement park rides, take a trip in the Space Needle's glass elevator (▶ 30) or visit museums and galleries, including the Children's Museum (▶ 60), Experience Music Project (▶ 31), several craft galleries, and the Pacific Science Center (▶ 29). Seattle Center is also home to opera, ballet, four excellent theater companies (▶ 78), and several professional sports teams. If you're hungry, stop in the Center House for a variety of eating choices; neighbourhood restaurants are close by.

Easy walking Stroll through the delightful Sculpture Garden and the adjacent Peace Garden southwest of the Needle. Enjoy a picnic on the grass by the International Fountain and watch children catch the spray on summer days.

INFORMATION

Monorail to Seattle Center

➕ E6

✉ Station at Westlake Center; Runs on 5th N to Seattle Center

☎ Seattle Center: 206/684–7200

🔄 Monorail: Runs daily every 15 minutes. Seattle Center grounds: year-round, Mon-Fri 7:30–11PM; Sat/Sun 9–11PM

🍴 Seattle Center House food concessions (Sun–Thu: 11–6; Fri/Sat: 11–8; closed Thanksgiving, Christmas, and New Year)

🚌 3, 4, 6

♿ Free to Center ground

The monorail station at Westlake Center

13

SEATTLE ART MUSEUM

People have strong reactions to the Seattle Art Museum building—they either love it or hate it. Whatever your taste in architecture, the museum's collections are sure to transport you in space and time.

Into another world The pink granite arcaded structure of the Seattle Art Museum (SAM), which opened in 1991, steps up the hill between 1st and 2nd Avenues. To reach the galleries, you ascend a grand staircase, walking the gauntlet between monumental paired rams, guardian figures, and sacred camels from the Ming dynasty.

Dazzling collections SAM's permanent collections range from the indigenous art of Africa, Oceania, and the Americas to modern U.S. paintings and sculpture. You will find works by Roy Lichtenstein, Andy Warhohl, Jackson Pollock, Max Beckman, as well as examples of works by artists of the 1950s Northwest School and other prominent artists of the region. The Katherine White collection of African sculpture, masks, textiles, and decorative arts is beautifully displayed, while a North-west Coast collection features small items, such as baskets and dream catchers, as well as much larger pieces, including four full-scale carved Kwakiutl house-posts. In other galleries, the museum presents traveling exhibitions and launches major shows of its own.

Hammering Man Like the museum itself, the 48-foot sculpture out front has invited controversy. Sculptor Jonathan Borofsky offers this justification: "I want this work to appeal to all people of Seattle—not just artists, but families young and old. At its heart, society reveres the worker. *The Hammering Man* is the worker in all of us."

LAKE UNION

In a neighborhood shared with tugboats and research ships, ducks and racoons, Lake Union's houseboaters gladly sacrifice dry land and backyards for a vibrant lifestyle on a bustling lake.

Floating world The houseboat life started over a century ago on Lake Union. A sawmill that opened on the lake in 1881 attracted a community of loggers and their hangers-on. Many of these woodsmen built themselves makeshift shelters by tying felled logs together and erecting tarpaper shacks on top. Before long, thousands of shacks floated on the waterways. These "floating homes," Seattle's earliest houseboats, were a far cry from the gentrified versions made familiar by the film *Sleepless in Seattle*.

Boats and shops Today Lake Union is a lively mix of marine activity, houseboat living, and expensive dining and shopping. Start your visit with a stroll, passing the 468-ton schooner *Wawona*, and the Center for Wooden Boats on the south end to get into the saltwater spirit. Then, for a true Lake Union experience, go out on the lake. You can rent sailboats, skiffs, or kayaks, and explore on your own (▶ 56–57), or sign on with a tour (▶ 19). Back ashore be sure to have a meal at one of the numerous good restaurants on Chandler's Cove.

DID YOU KNOW?

- Seattle has more houseboats than anywhere east of Asia, and most are on Lake Union
- Lake Union took its name from a pioneer's speech in which he dreamed that one day, a lake would form "the union" between Puget Sound and Lake Washington
- Visitors who want to experience lakefront living can stay in a "bunk and breakfast" anchored in the lake
- Gasworks Park on the north side offers great views of downtown and is the city's premiere kite-flying spot

INFORMATION

- 70, 71, 72, 73 on Fairview/Eastlake
- Kayak, rowboat, and sailboat rentals (▶ 56–57), Argosy Lake tours and "Discover Houseboating" tours (▶ 19), Seattle Seaplanes and Kenmore Air (▶ 19)

A "street" of houseboat homes on Lake Union

15

DOWNTOWN

These days, downtown is jumping. Old buildings have resurfaced as theaters and shops, and Seattle's boom continues to spawn new stores, restaurants, hotels, and entertainment venues.

Getting your bearings The phrase "Downtown Seattle" is a rather ambiguous term that usually refers to a large area encompassing the Denny Regrade (Belltown), Pike Place Market, Pioneer Square, and the International District. Seattle's retail core, however, is concentrated roughly in the center, between University and Stewart, and between 3rd and 7th Avenues. Most shops, restaurants, hotels, and travel offices are clustered in and around Westlake Center, City Centre, Rainier Square, and Union Square.

Shopping Triangular Westlake Park, with its public art and curtain of water, is a popular gathering place, especially when steel bands are jamming. Across the square, Westlake Center lures shoppers with its food court and specialty shops. South of Westlake, chain stores like Niketown, FAO Schwartz, and Banana Republic (➤ 70) have moved in, while a state-of-the-art video arcade, 16-screen theater, and Planet Hollywood offer contemporary entertainment nearby. Also check out City Centre's exclusive shops, the Palomino Bistro (at 5th Avenue and Pike), and The Sharper Image, an emporium devoted to high-tech gadgets. At 5th and Union, you'll pass Eddie Bauer (➤ 70), America's first outdoor retailer. Across the street, the Security Pacific Bank Tower (➤ 54) houses Rainier Square with its three-story atrium and specialty shops.

If you're ready for tea or a snack, stop in at the Four Seasons Olympic Garden Court, across the street, or grab some fresh oysters at Shuckers.

PIONEER SQUARE

Pioneer Square's distinctive brick buildings were constructed after the Great Seattle Fire, and give this neighborhood an architectural integrity you won't find elsewhere in the city.

From the ashes In 1852, Seattle's pioneers moved across Elliott Bay and built the first permanent settlement in what is now Pioneer Square. The area burned to the ground in 1889, but was quickly rebuilt. When gold was discovered in the Yukon, prospectors converged on Pioneer Square to board ships to Alaska, and the area became miners' primary outfitting post for.

Moving through the square Pioneer Square's most notable landmarks include Smith Tower (► 54) and the lovely glass-and-iron pergola at 1st and Yesler. Interesting shops lining 1st Avenue between Yesler and Jackson include the Flying Shuttle and the Gallery of Fine Woodworking (► 73). Also worth a visit are the shops inside Grand Central Arcade, which opens onto Occidental Park. Continue south along Occidental's mall, taking time to visit the Klondike Gold Rush National Historic Park. Around the corner is enchanting Waterfall Park, and two blocks west, the Elliott Bay Book Company invites browsing. Dine at one of the area's excellent restaurants, catch some live music, or head for laughs at the Comedy Underground.

HIGHLIGHTS

- The pergola at 1st and Yesler
- Smith Tower
- Shops lining 1st Avenue and inside Grand Central Arcade
- Occidental Park and totem poles
- Klondike Gold Rush National Historic Park
- Waterfall Park
- The Elliott Bay Book Company bookstore

INFORMATION

Pioneer Square
- G6
- Area: from Yesler to King and 2nd Avenue to Elliot Bay; Visitor Information booth in Occidental Mall during summer

Klondike Gold Rush National Historic Park
- 117 S. Main
- 206/553–7220
- Daily 9–5
- Buses on 1st and 2nd Avenues (free-ride zone). Waterfront trolley stop
- Wheelchair access
- Free
- Waterfront (► 32), International District (► 41), Seattle Art Museum (► 36), Pike Place Market (► 33), Harbor Steps (► 54)

Nineteenth-century red-brick elegance at Pioneer Square

REI (Recreational Equipment Inc.)

DID YOU KNOW?

- Lou Whittaker, general manager in the 1950s, was the first American to climb Everest
- REI is the largest retail co-operative in the United States, with over 1.4 million members
- The new REI building was constructed with materials that are either recycled or have minimal impact on the environment
- The Seattle store's 65-foot climbing pinnacle is the world's highest

INFORMATION

- ✚ D4
- ✉ 222 Yale Avenue North
- ☎ 206/223–1944
- ◷ Mon–Sat 10–9; Sun 11–6
- 🍴 World Wraps on site
- 🚌 70, 25
- ♿ Good
- ❓ Pinnacle to climb (fee for non-members); educational programs; equipment repair

The massive popularity of Recreational Equipment Inc., Seattle's premier retailer of outdoor wear and equipment, is legendary. The annual garage sale draws hordes of devotees who gather like pilgrims at a holy shrine.

It began with an ice axe REI had humble origins in the 1930s. It was founded by Seattle climber Lloyd Anderson, whose search for a high-quality, affordable ice axe ended in frustration—the one he wanted was not sold in the United States but could be ordered only from Europe. Anderson purchased one and soon his climbing buddies wanted their own. In 1938, 23 climbers banded together to form a member-owned co-operative in order to obtain mountaineering equipment unavailable in the United States.

Try it out REI's new store is *the* place to try before you buy. Under staff guidance, you can, for example, don a harness and scale the store's free-standing 65-foot high indoor pinnacle. The store also has its own hiking trail, where you can test the toughness of boots on uneven terrain; another trail designed for mountain-bike test rides; and a "rain room" where you can test the water-proof claims of the wide variety of outerwear.

Try out your skills and test the gear on the store's climbing pinnacle

THE INTERNATIONAL DISTRICT

Seattle's International District is home to the city's Chinese, Japanese, Filipino, Southeast Asian, Korean, and other Asian communities.

Multicultural mix The first Asian people to arrive in Seattle were Chinese men, who moved north from California to build the railways. Anti-Chinese riots broke out in the 1880s and many Chinese were deported, only to return after 1889 to help rebuild the charred settlement. The Japanese arrived next, many establishing small farms and selling their goods at Pike Place Market. The Filipinos, the third group to arrive, now constitute Seattle's largest Asian community.

The neighborhood Smaller and more modest than San Francisco's Chinatown, the International District caters primarily to those who live and work in the neighborhood. Consequently, it feels more genuine than equivalent areas in cities that attract more tourists. It is comprised mainly of old buildings, often with markets, Chinese apothecaries, restaurants, or family associations on the ground floor, and lodgings upstairs. A good place to start to explore the district is the Wing Luke Asian Museum. Pick up a walking map, and include in your travels Hing Hay Park and Uwajimaya, the largest Asian emporium in the Northwest.

Eat city The district has many excellent Asian restaurants. Good bets include House of Hong or Sun-Ya for dim sum. Or have a Chinese lunch or dinner at Shanghai Garden or Hing Loon, or noodles at the Cambodian Phnom Penh Noodle House. For Japanese fare, try Mikado, Kaizuka, Ichiban, or Takohachi; for Vietnamese, go to Viet My (near 4th and Washington), Huong Binh, or the NHK Malaysian Restaurant in Little Saigon at 12th and Jackson.

HIGHLIGHTS

- The many Asian restaurants
- Wing Luke Museum
- Hing Hay Park, with its ornate pavilion and dragon mural
- Uwajimaya, a large Asian emporium

INFORMATION

The International District
- ✚ E4, F4
- ✉ Between S Main and Lane Street and 5th and 8th Avenue S; "Little Saigon" 12th S and Jackson.

Wing Luke Asian Museum
- ✉ 407 Seventh Ave S
- ☎ 206/623–5124
- 🕐 Tue, Wed, Fri 11–4:30; Thu 11–7; Sat/Sun 12–4
- 🚌 1, 7 and 14 to Maynard and Jackson. Waterfront trolley to Jackson Street Station
- ♿ Wheelchair access for Museum only
- 💲 Inexpensive; free Thu
- ↔ Pioneer Square (▶ 39)
- ❓ Chinese New Year celebration in February

19

VOLUNTEER PARK

DID YOU KNOW?

- The park began to assume its present form in 1904
- The water tower is 75 feet high
- The Seattle Asian Art Museum was collector Richard Fuller's gift to Seattle in 1932

INFORMATION

Volunteer Park

- ➕ C4, C5
- ✉ Between E. Galer and E. Prospect and 15th and 11th Avenues
- ☎ 206/625–8901
- 🕐 Park open daily, dawn to dusk. Conservatory, daily: summer, 10–7; otherwise 10–4
- 🎫 Free
- 🚌 10, 7
- ♿ Poor

Seattle Asian Art Museum

- ☎ 206/625–8900
- 🕐 Tue–Sun 10–5 except Thu, 10–9; closed Mon except holiday Mondays; closed Thanksgiving, Christmas, New Year's.
- ♿ Fair
- 🎫 Moderate; free first Thu and Sat of month, and first Fri for seniors. Free with SAM admission ticket

Above: The view from Volunteer Park's water tower

In Volunteer Park there are not only the requisite gardens, grassy lawns, and towering trees, but also a water tower to climb for views, a conservatory and Seattle's prized Asian Art Museum.

Seattle Asian Art Museum (SAAM) Carl Gould's art deco building once housed the entire Seattle Art Museum (SAM) collection (► 36). In 1991 SAM moved into a new downtown building, leaving the Volunteer Park museum to focus exclusively on Asian art. The extensive Chinese collection includes ancient burial ceramics, ritual bronzes, snuff bottles, and a lovely Chinese Buddhist room, whose serene gray walls set off the gilded sculptures. Here you'll find the wonderful *Monk Caught at the Moment of Enlightenment*. SAAM also contains Korean, South, and Southeast Asian collections, as well as a notable Japanese gallery which features a portion of an early 17th-century "deer scroll," considered a Japanese national treasure. SAAM offers Sunday afternoon concerts and dance programs, often in the central Garden Court. After touring the museum, you can sample your choice of teas in the Kado Tearoom.

Outside the museum Volunteer Park was named during the Spanish-American War of 1898 to honor those who had served as soldiers. Climb the water tower for a splendid 360-degree view, or stroll through the graceful Conservatory, where thousands of plants in five separate rooms simulate botanical environments from around the world. In winter, there's nothing like stepping into the tropics room, filled with giant ferns, palms, and orchids. Just north of the park boundaries at Lakeview Cemetery, you can pay tribute at the graves of actor and martial arts legend Bruce Lee and his son, Brandon.

MUSEUM OF FLIGHT

This is quite simply the finest air and space museum on the West Coast. Even technophobes will be engaged and delighted.

Flight path The 185,075-square foot Museum of Flight is on the southwest corner of Boeing Field and King County International Airport, and is partly housed in the original Red Barn, where the Boeing Company built its first planes.

Great Gallery The Red Barn exhibit documents early aviation up to 1938, while the airy and breathtaking Great Gallery traces the story of flight from early mythology to the latest accomplishments in space. Overhead, more than 20 full-sized airplanes hang at varying levels from a ceiling grid. All face the same direction, like a squadron frozen in flight. Another exhibit contains artifacts from the Apollo space program, including an Apollo command module, lunar rocks, and the Lunar Roving Vehicle. The museum also has a full-sized air traffic control tower. Like a working tower, this simulated version overlooks airport runways and has overhead speakers that broadcast air traffic transmissions. Outside the museum building, you can tour the original Air Force One presidential jet.

You be the pilot In the fascinating Tower Exhibit, you can pilot an imaginary flight from Denver to Seattle to witness the behind-the-scenes work of air traffic controllers. Through visual cues on a radar screen and telephone instructions, you can perform the numerous tasks required to fly the plane, from checking weather data and filing a flight plan to landing.

HIGHLIGHTS

- A restored 1917 Curtiss "Jenny" biplane, Charles Lindbergh's first plane
- A flying replica of the B&W, Boeing's first plane
- The only MD-21 Blackbird spy plane in existence
- Apollo space program artifacts
- A full-sized air traffic control tower
- Piloting an imaginary flight

INFORMATION

- M3
- 9404 E.Marginal Way South by Boeing Field (I-5 exit 158)
- 206/764–5720
- 10–5; Thu 10–9
- Wings Café, open museum hours
- 174
- Excellent
- Moderate
- Guided half and one-hour museum tours; lectures, concerts, films, and special events

A 1917 Curtiss "Jenny"

21

UNIVERSITY OF WASHINGTON

DID YOU KNOW?

- Most locals call the university "U Dub"
- Suzzalo & Allen Library was modeled after King's College Chapel in Cambridge, England
- Husky Stadium has seats for 72,000 people

INFORMATION

- A5, A6
- Between 15th and 25th Avenue, NE and Campus Parkway, and NE 45th Street; (UW Visitor Center, Mon–Fri, 4014 Univeristy Way NE at Campus Parkway)
- 206/543–9198, Visitor Center
- 70, 71, 72, 73, 43, 25
- Good
- Henry Art Gallery (► 45), Burke Museum (► 46), U District (► 55), Arboretum (► 47), Museum of History and Industry (► 52)

Above: Part of the university campus. The Cascade Mountains are on the horizon

The original University of Washington grounds, extensively remodeled by the Olmsted Brothers, for a 1909 exposition, includes Rainier Vista—a concourse framing Mt. Rainier—and Frosh Pond, where Drumheller Fountain shoots water 30 feet into the air.

Vistas and fountains Established in 1861 on a site in the downtown area, the university moved to its present location 30 years later. To begin your tour stop at the Visitor Information Center to pick up a free self-guided walking tour map and an events schedule. As you walk, you'll see buildings in a variety of architectural styles, from turreted Denny Hall to cathedral-like Suzzalo & Allen Library. The Suzallo & Allen faces Red Square, a student gathering place. Only the Broken Obelisk sculpture and three campanile towers break the horizontal line of this plaza, which is bordered by Meany Hall, a performing arts venue.

Elsewhere To the west, lies the Henry Art Gallery (► 45). To the north, the old campus quadrangle is especially inviting in late March or early April when rows of pink Japanese cherry trees burst into bloom. Continuing toward the university's north entrance, you come to the Burke Museum (► 46) and UW's observatory, which is open to the public. If you head toward the Waterfront Activities building, you can rent a canoe and paddle on Lake Washington.

The Ave One block west of the campus lies University Avenue Northeast, known as "the Ave," the main drag through the "U district." Here, a multitude of ethnic restaurants alternate with excellent booksellers, secondhand stores, and import shops.

HENRY ART GALLERY

Greatly enhanced by a striking addition to the building, this is Seattle's leading venue for cutting-edge art.

The new Henry The Henry Art Gallery reopened in 1997 with a greatly increased floor space. Architect Charles Gwathmey has created a series of windows and skylights that bring natural light into the building. By building into the side of the hill, Gwathmey has managed to preserve both the Henry's original 1927 facade and easterly views over the university campus. The luminous new South Gallery is an ideal space for traveling exhibitions and installations.

The collection Works from the permanent collection are exhibited on a rotating basis in the old building's North Gallery. A cornerstone of the collection is the Monsen Collection of Photography, prized for its scope, from vintage prints to contemporary explorations of the medium. The permanent collection also includes late 19th- and early 20th-century landscape painting; modern art by Stuart Davis, Robert Motherwell, Jacob Lawrence, and Lionel Feininger; examples from the Northwest School; and an extensive Native American textile collection.

Learn as you go The Henry has a particular commitment to art education, offering several free programs for both adults and children. Twice monthly at 12:15 the gallery presents Midday Art Moments, when curatorial staff and distinguished guests speak informally about the current exhibitions. One evening a month, during Thursday's free evening hours, you can participate in Art Dialogues, lively discussions of current shows with University of Washington staff and other special guests. These meet in one of the galleries at 7PM. Other events include lectures, and children's art workshops.

HIGHLIGHTS

- The Monsen Collection of Photography
- Regular artists' lectures, symposia, and film showings
- Special hands-on workshops for children one Saturday a month

INFORMATION

- A5
- UW campus at 15th Avenue. NE and NE 41st Street
- 206/543–2280 (recorded information); 543–2281 for scheduled tours/events.
- Tue–Sun 11–5 except 11–8 Thu. Closed Mon and July 4, Thanksgiving, Christmas, and New Year's
- Gallery café
- 70, 71, 72, 73, 43, 25
- Very good
- Moderate; Free Thu, 5–8
- University of Washington (➤ 44), Burke Museum (➤ 46), U District (➤ 55), Arboretum (➤ 47), Museum of History and Industry (➤ 52)
- Tours, lectures, and discussions, special events; gallery store

BURKE MUSEUM

The Burke's permanent exhibits demonstrate at once a keen artistic sense, deep respect for the cultural traditions of featured groups, and a scientist's attention to detail. It's a rare combination.

The Burke's beginnings The museum's origins date back to 1879, when four enthusiastic teenagers calling themselves the Young Naturalists set about collecting Northwest plant and animal specimens, a popular hobby at the time. Their collection grew, so much so that to house it a museum was built on the University of Washington campus in 1885. Over the next 20 years, the number of specimens increased, and today, they form the basis of the Burke's extensive collection, which totals more than three million objects. The museum moved into its current building in 1962.

Treasures on display As you walk through the entrance, a stunning glass display case demands immediate attention. It highlights selected treasures from this vast collection, and gives you an idea of what's in store. In the halls beyond, two new exhibits showcase the museum's strong suits: natural history and ethnography. The Pacific Voices exhibit conveys the variety and richness of Pacific Rim cultures, from New Zealand to the northwest coast of Canada. By framing the exhibit around the celebrations and rituals that are central to each culture, museum artifacts are placed within their appropriate context. Constructed "sets," photo murals, recorded sounds, and informative text bring objects to life and communicate the importance of cultural traditions. The Life and Times of Washington State exhibit is a chronological journey through 545 million years of Washington natural history.

DID YOU KNOW?

- The museum's anthropological division has the largest Northwest Coast collection of Indian artifacts in the western United States
- The 37,000 bird specimens in the ornithology collection account for 95 percent of North American species
- Before the Burke opened, a number of ethnic groups came to the museum for private "blessing" ceremonies to consecrate their installations

INFORMATION

- ⊞ B6
- ✉ University of Washington campus at NE 45th Street and 17th Avenue NE
- ☎ 206/543–5590 (Recording), 206/543–7907 (exhibit/special events)
- 🕐 Daily 10–5 except Thu, 10–8
- 🍴 Burke Café
- 🚍 71, 72, 73, 43
- ♿ Very good
- 💰 Moderate
- ↔ University of Washington (➤ 44), Burke Museum (➤ 46), U District (➤ 55), Arboretum (➤ 47), Museum of History and Industry (➤ 52)
- ❓ Tours, lectures, children's workshops, special events; museum shop

WASHINGTON PARK ARBORETUM

This large botanical collection owes its origins to Edmond S. Meany, founder of the University of Washington's School of Forestry. Meany initiated a seed exchange with universities around the world, and today's garden combines these exotics with virtually every woodland plant indigenous to the area.

Green oasis In this pretty arboretum you can walk among a variety of ecological zones, from woodland to marshland.

The Japanese Garden On the west side of Lake Washington Boulevard, tucked away behind a wooden fence, lies the restful Japanese Garden. Elements of the garden—plants, trees, water, rocks—and their placement, represent a miniature world of mountain, forest, lake, river, and tableland. There's also a ceremonial teahouse.

Waterfront trail This 1½-mile trail, originating behind the Museum of History and Industry (➤ 52), winds through marshland on floating platforms and footbridges. At Foster Island, it cuts under the Evergreen Point Floating Bridge and continues through what was once a Native American burial ground to Duck Pond. To experience this convergence of man and nature from the water, rent a canoe (➤ 56) and go for a paddle through water-lilies among the mallards and their ducklings.

DID YOU KNOW?

- Arboretum area: 200 acres
- Botanist Edmond S. Meany test-planted imported seeds in his own garden, and later transplanted the plants on campus
- The Japanese Garden was designed in 1960 by Juki Iida, a Tokyo landscape architect, who personally supervized both its planning and construction

INFORMATION

- ✚ B6, C6
- ✉ Between E. Madison Street and Hwy 520, and 26th Avenue E and Arboretum Drrive E (Graham Visitor's Center at 2300 Arboretum Drive E)
- ☎ 206/543–8800
- 🕐 Daily from 8AM to sunset; Japanese Garden open Apr–Oct
- 🚌 11
- ♿ None
- 🎟 Free for waterfront and woodland trails; fee for Japanese Garden
- ↔ Museum of History and Industry (➤ 52), University of Washington (➤ 44)
- ❓ Free one-hour guided tours, year-round, Sat–Sun at 1

THE BOEING TOUR

- Boeing now owns Rockwell, contractor for the U.S. space shuttle, and McDonnell Douglas, manufacturer of the DC9
- Boeing workers use bicycles to get around the factory floor
- Boeing offers buyers a range of customized interiors. The new 747-400s for Saudi Arabian Airlines provide curtained prayer rooms equipped with electronic devices pointing to Mecca

INFORMATION

- ✚ J3
- ✉ Tour Center off Hwy 189 West (via I-5 northbound)
- ☎ 206/544–1264 (recording); 800/464–1746
- 🕐 Mon–Fri hourly, 9, 10–3 during the summer; twice or more daily, winter. Closed weekends. Call for holiday closure schedule. Gray Line of Seattle tours (206/626–5208; 800/426–7532)
- ♿ Very good
- ✋ Free
- ❓ Tickets distributed at 8:30AM for same day tours. Arrive early during peak season—individual admission on first-come basis (admission guaranteed for Gray Line bus tours); gift store

Over the years, Seattle's fortunes have soared and dipped on the wings of Boeing. Touring the 747 plant and seeing workers on the job puts a human face on the region's largest employer.

Ceaseless activity Thirty minutes north of Seattle, in the world's largest building measured by volume, 32,000 employees go about the intricate process of assembling wide body jets. Here, 747s, 767s and the newest, the 777, are assembled around the clock.

The tour The 90-minute Boeing tour begins with a short film. Afterwards, a guide takes you to the plant's third floor, where an observation deck gives a view of the final 747 assembly operation. Outside, you are shown where the painting, fueling, and ground testing of the aircraft occurs.

Boeing's fortunes After flying with a barnstorming pilot at a 1915 flight show, young William Boeing was convinced of two things: that he could build a better plane, and that aviation was destined for more than mere entertainment. In 1916, with the help of his friend, naval architect Conrad Westerveld, he built the B&W, the first Boeing aircraft. The young company struggled on the verge of bankruptcy following World War I, manufacturing bedroom furniture to stay afloat. Boeing's boom years commenced with the design and manufacture of the B-17 bomber, used by the Allies in the attacks on Germany. Company fortunes continued to soar through the Cold War until 1969, when severe recession hit. Thousands of workers were laid off leading someone to pen this tongue-in-cheek message on a downtown billboard: "Will the last Boeing employee to leave Seattle please turn out the lights?"

SEATTLE's *best*

49

PARKS & BEACHES

The green city

The city's 300 or so parks are often cited as key to Seattle's liveability. Credit goes to city officials, who feared that unchecked logging would destroy Seattle's natural beauty, and to Chicago's Olmsted Brothers Landscape Architects, who were hired to draft a comprehensive plan for the city in 1903. The system of parks and connecting boulevards they designed forms the backbone of Seattle's 5,000 acres of parkland.

See Top 25 Sights for
ALKI BEACH (► 25)
DISCOVERY PARK & DAYBREAK STAR ART CENTER (► 24)
THE HIRAM M CHITTENDEN LOCKS (► 26)
VOLUNTEER PARK (► 42)
WASHINGTON PARK ARBORETUM (► 47)
WOODLAND PARK ZOO (► 28)
See Evening Strolls for
GREEN LAKE (► 18)
MYRTLE EDWARDS/ELLIOTT BAY PARK (► 18)

FREEWAY PARK

When Freeway Park opened in 1976, it won national attention for the ingenious way it created an urban oasis over ten lanes of freeway. The design called for a concrete "lid" over Interstate 5, pollution-resistant trees, and a waterfall thundering at a rate of 27,000 gallons a minute to mask traffic noise. Note George Tsutakawa's handsome bronze fountain.

➕ F6 ✉ 6th Ave and Seneca St, south of Washington State Convention Center 🚌 2

GASWORKS PARK

This park on north Lake Union is popular for picnics, kite-flying, and skateboarding, with it's wonderful views of downtown. Rusted, graffiti-marked towers and brightly painted machinery in the play area recall this site's origins as a gas plant. Climb the grassy mound to see the park's sundial or to launch a kite.

➕ B3 ✉ N Northlake Way and Meridian Ave N 🚌 26

GOLDEN GARDENS BEACH PARK

This beach park is teen heaven: you'll find a half-mile strip of sandy beach and trail, views of the Olympics, a bathhouse, concessions, picnic shelters, and firepits. And if yachts are your thing, check out the ones next door, at Shilshloe Marina A walk along the beach at dusk is a must.

➕ K2 ✉ Seaview Ave 🚌 17, 86

Gasworks Park

KERRY VIEWPOINT

This tiny park on Queen Anne hill has a great view of downtown and features Doris Chase's steel sculpture *Changing Form*.

➕ C2 ✉ W Highland Drive and 2nd W 🚌 2 or 13

LINCOLN PARK

In this lovely West Seattle park south of Alki, you'll find something for everyone: great views, rocky beaches with tidepools, walking and biking trails, picnic shelters, tennis courts, a horseshoe pit, a children's playground, and Seattle's only outdoor saltwater pool and waterslide.

➕ M2 ✉ Fauntleroy Ave SW and SW Webster 🚌 54

MADISON PARK

In this neighborhood beach park on the western shore of Lake Washington, you can sunbathe on a grassy slope. There's a bathhouse and a swimming dock with diving board (lifeguards in summer).

➕ C6 ✉ The foot of E Madison St at 43rd Avenue E 🚌 11

MATTHEWS BEACH

At this swimming beach on the north shore of Lake Washington, bikers on the 16½ mile lakeside Burke-Gilman trail stop to cool down or enjoy a picnic on the grassy meadows. There's also a playground for the children.

➕ K3 ✉ NE 93rd off Sand Point Way NE 🚌 74, 74

SEWARD PARK

This beautiful 277-acre wilderness on the south shore of Lake Washington has a beach and trails along the waterfront and through old-growth cedar and fir forest (where it is sometimes possible to catch views of the two pairs of nesting eagles). It's a wonderful place for a picnic, especially if you come via bicycle on a Bicycle Saturday or Sunday, when Lake Washington is closed to traffic. Also features a fish hatchery and picnic shelters with barbecues.

➕ L3 ✉ Lake Washington Boulevard S and S Juneau 🚌 39

Seattle area beaches

With several freshwater lakes and miles of shoreline along Elliott Bay, Seattle boasts a number of beach parks within its city limits. However, in Seattle the term "beach" is not necessarily synonymous with "swimming." Few choose to swim in the chilly waters of Puget Sound, apart from a quick dash in and out on a hot summer's day. The freshwater of Greenlake and Lake Washington, on the other hand, are pleasant for more extended swims.

Golden Gardens Beach Park, backed by the snow-capped Olympic Mountains

51

MUSEUMS

Asian heritage

The Wing Luke Museum in the International District presents the history and traditions of the Asian and Pacific Island groups that have settled in the area. Two permanent installations employ photographs, artifacts, text, and video to tell the story. The museum center is at 417 7th Avenue South
(☎ 206/623–5124).

See Top 25 Sights for
BURKE MUSEUM OF NATURAL HISTORY & CULTURE (► 46)
EXPERIENCE MUSIC PROJECT ► 31)
HENRY ART GALLERY (► 45)
KLONDIKE GOLD RUSH NATIONAL HISTORIC PARK(► 39)
MUSEUM OF FLIGHT (► 43)
PACIFIC SCIENCE CENTER (► 29)
SEATTLE ART MUSEUM (► 36)
SEATTLE ASIAN ART MUSEUM (► 42)

FRYE ART MUSEUM

This beautiful, spacious gallery devoted to representational art rotates works from the permanent collection, most notably pieces by William Merritt Chase, Winslow Homer, John Singer Sargeant, and Renoir.

➕ E4 ✉ 704 Terry Avenue ☎ 206/622–9250 🍴 Café on site 🚌 3, 4 (on 3rd Avenue) ❓ Sun afternoon concerts ♿ Excellent ✋ Free

MUSEUM OF HISTORY AND INDUSTRY (MOHAI)

Two new exhibits have made this small museum a lively learning center: Salmon Stakes brings the early canning industry to life; in Seattle Roots you assume a pioneer identity and follow your character along a 19th century Seattle street.

➕ B5 ✉ 2700 24th Avenue E, south of the Montlake Bridge ☎ 206/324–1126 🕐 Tue–Fri,11–5, Sat–Sun 10–5; closed Thanksgiving, Christmas, New Year, and Mon except holiday Mons 🚌 25, 43 and 48 ♿ Excellent ✋ Moderate

An old salmon advertisement, Museum of History and Industry

NORDIC HERITAGE MUSEUM

This is the only museum in the United States to showcase the heritage of all five Nordic nations: Denmark, Finland, Iceland, Norway, and Sweden. In the Dream of America exhibit you follow the immigrant experience: departure, crossing, a new land, and the industries in which immigrants played important roles, especially logging and fishing. Five other galleries tell the unique story of each Nordic group. The museum also presents excellent contemporary art exhibitions and cultural events.

➕ G1 ✉ 3014 NW 67th Street ☎ 206/789-5707 🕐 Tue–Sun 🚌 17 (on 4th Avenue) ✋ Inexpensive; free first Tue of month

PUBLIC ART

A SOUND GARDEN
One of Seattle's small treasures. Doug Hollis's work consists of 12 steel towers supporting wind activated organ pipes that create gentle sounds on windy days.
➕ C4 ✉ Behind NOAA building, 7600 Standpoint Way NE 🚍 71, 72

BUS TUNNEL ART
Artists worked with architects and engineers on the design for five underground stations: Convention Place, Westlake, University, Pioneer Square, and the International District. The design reflects the character of each neighborhood.
🕐 Closed Sun

DANCERS' SERIES: STEPS
At each of eight locations, Jack Mackie has fashioned cast bronze shoeprints in the pattern of a couple's feet as they dance the tango, waltz, lindy, fox trot, rhumba, and mambo.
✉ Broadway on Capitol Hill 🚍 7

FREMONT TROLL
This whimsical giant, who is crushing a real Volkswagen Bug with his bare hand, is both a reference to Scandinavian folklore and an expression of Fremont's collective sense of humor.
➕ A3 ✉ N 36th St under the Aurora Avenue Bridge 🚍 26, 28

OCCIDENTAL PARK TOTEMS
Duane Pasco's painted cedar logs—*Sun and Raven, Tsonqua,* and *Killer Whale and Bear*—date from 1975.
➕ G6 ✉ Occidental Park, Occidental Ave S and S Main in Pioneer Square 🚍 Buses on 1st in free zone

WAITING FOR THE INTERURBAN
Richard Beyer's sculpture is a much-loved fixture of Fremont. Rarely are these gray aluminum trolley riders unadorned, either with scarves and hats in winter, or through the year with balloons to acknowledge someone's birthday.
➕ A3 ✉ Fremont Ave N and N 34th St 🚍 26, 28

Public Art

From manhole covers and benches to bus tunnel tiles, public art is incorporated into the very fabric of Seattle's daily life. This phenonemon stems from the city's May 1973 "One Percent for Art" ordinance, which specifies that 1 percent of all new municipal improvement funds must be set aside for the purchase and installation of public art. At least half of all allocations are awarded to artists residing in the Pacific Northwest. After an open call for applications selection is finalized after a review by a Seattle Arts Commission panel.

The troll at Fremont

ARCHITECTURE

CHAPEL OF ST. IGNATIUS

This sublime chapel is Seattle University's architectural gift to the city. Architect Steven Holl visualized the structure as "seven bottles of light in a stone box," with light bouncing off the tinted baffles to create a halo effect on surrounding walls.

The ornate interior of the Fifth Avenue Theater

➕ E4 ✉ 12th Avenue near Marion on Capitol Hill 🕐 Mon–Thu 7AM–10PM, Fri 7–7, Sat 9–5, Sun 9–11. Regular liturgies ☎ 206/296-6075(106) 🚌 11

FIFTH AVENUE THEATER

Ornately carved inside, the theater is patterned after the imperial throne room in Beijing's Forbidden City.
➕ F6 ✉ 1308 5th Avenue ☎ 206/625-1900 🚌 Downtown free zone buses along 1st to 4th Avenue

HARBOR STEPS

In creating a pedestrian link between the Waterfront and 1st Avenue Vancouver architect Arthur Anderson crafted an inviting urban plaza with waterfalls, seating, and plantings.
➕ F6 ✉ University Avenue 🚌 Downtown free zone buses along 1st to 4th Avenue

SECURITY PACIFIC BANK TOWER

Architect Minoru Yamasaki once said that he tried to create "delight, serenity, and surprise" in his buildings. This inverted white pencil, balanced on a 12-story base, clearly succeeds at least on the last count.
➕ F6 ✉ 1200 4th Avenue between Union and University 🚌 Downtown free zone buses along 1st to 4th Avenue

WASHINGTON MUTUAL BUILDING

As critics lambasted this late 1980s Kohn Pederson Fox building as an Empire State clone, the public applauded the post-modern style as relief from the cold glass boxes that dominate downtown.
➕ F6 ✉ 1201 3rd Avenue 🚌 Downtown free zone buses along 1st to 4th Avenue

Smith Tower

When it opened in 1914, Smith Tower was Seattle's first steel-framed skyscraper and the tallest building outside of New York City. At 42 stories, it remained the tallest building west of the Mississippi until 1969. For a modest fee, you can ride to the 35th floor in the company of the last of Seattle's elevator attendants to get a sweeping view of downtown.

✉ 506 2nd Ave and Yesler Way

Neighborhoods

Fremont follies

Seattle has earned its "most liveable city" moniker through the strength and character of its neighborhoods, of which Fremont, where tongue-in-cheek irreverence runs high, ranks as the quirkiest. In Fremont, bumper-stickers that elsewhere in the United States read: "HONK IF YOU LOVE JESUS;" instead ask you to: "HONK IF YOU *ARE* JESUS."

BELLTOWN
This unconventional neighborhood north of the Market is an odd mix of seediness and gentrification. The area's working-class roots are still evident even as upscale restaurants and condos, cyber-cafés, and taverns with art on the walls have transformed and energized the neighborhood.
🚌 Buses on 1st and 3rd

CAPITOL HILL
Diverse and progressive, 2 miles east of downtown, it's the focal point of the Seattle gay community, and home to a smattering of Seattle's monied elite as well as tattooed teens, young professionals, and seniors on fixed incomes. The action is concentrated along Broadway in cafés, restaurants, retro shops, and clubs.
🚌 7 to Broadway E, or 10 to 15th Avenue E

FREMONT
This offbeat neighborhood, which proclaims itself a republic and "the Center of the Universe," is known for its tolerance and quirky humor. Check out the public art, from the monumental statue of Lenin to the Volkswagen-crushing Fremont Troll under Aurora Bridge.
🚌 26, 28

MADISON PARK
This older residential neighborhood bordering Lake Washington at the foot of Madison boasts lovely homes, a popular beach and a cluster of interesting specialty shops and cafés.
🚌 11 to the foot of Madison

Artistic graffiti in Fremont

THE UNIVERSITY DISTRICT
This area includes the University of Washington (► 44), "the Ave," and University Village, a complex of tasteful specialty shops, markets, and cafes. "The Ave" is all student haunts and the awesome and justifiably renowned University Bookstore.
🚌 Many including 7, 43, 70, 71, 72, 73, 85

ACTIVE PURSUITS

See Evening Strolls for
GREEN LAKE (▶ 18)
MYRTLE EDWARDS/ELLIOTT BAY PARK (▶ 18)
See Parks and Beaches for
**MADISON PARK, MATTHEWS BEACH, SEWARD
PARK (▶ 50–51)**

Seattle by bike

Despite the omnipresent threat of drizzle and the challenge of hilly terrain, growing numbers of Seattleites are taking to two wheels for commuting and recreation. The city is laced with bike trails, including a number of flat, scenic routes that reward bikers and in-line skaters with spectacular views.

BIKE TRAILS

• Alki Beach to Lincoln Park: This bikeway is marked only part of the way, continuing along the shoreline to Lincoln Park will give you a 12-mile round trip. (Flat.)
🚌 37

• Burke-Gilman Trail: This level, paved lakeside trail follows an old railroad right-of-way for 16½ miles, skirting Fremont, Wallingford, and the University of Washington campus. From Fremont/Ballard at the southwest end, the trail runs east along the ship canal, Lake Union, and Portage Bay. At the University of Washington's Husky Stadium, the trail swings north along Lake Washington and continues for 12 miles to the northern tip of the lake at the town of Kenmore. If you want to go to the Woodinville Wineries and Brewpub, pick up the Sammamish River Trail. (Flat.)

• Lake Washington Boulevard. In summer on Bicycle Saturdays and Sundays, traffic is barred from a 6-mile stretch of Lake Washington Boulevard, between the arboretum and

Exploring Seattle by bike

Lake Washington and south along the lake to Seward Park, is closed to traffic for the enjoyment of bicyclists. (Mostly flat; one steep hill.) This stretch connects with Seward Park's 2½ mile loop. (▶ 51)
☎ Bicycle Sat/Sun Schedule: 206/684-4075

• Magnolia Bluff Bike Trail: Three miles from Discovery Park to Magnolia Park with views of Elliott Bay, the Olympics, West Seattle, Mt. Rainier, and downtown. Moderate, one steep hill.
🚌 33

BIKE RENTALS

• Gregg's Green Lake Cycle. Also rents in-line skates.
➕ A6   7007 Woodlawn Ave NE ☎ 206/523–1822
• Magnolia Alpine Hut: rents bikes, in-line skates

and sit-on kayaks in summer; skis in winter.
🚼 B1 ✉ 2215 15th Ave W ☎ 206/284–3575 🕐 Mon–Fri 10–6;
Sat 10–5, Sun in winter: 12–5 🚌 15, 18
• Montlake Bicycle Shop
🚼 C5 ✉ 2223 24th Avenue E (near the Arboretum)
☎ 206/329–7333 🚌 43

BOAT RENTALS
• Green Lake Boat Rentals: paddleboats and
rowboats.
🚼 A6 ✉ 7351 E Green Lake Drive N
☎ 206/527–0171 🕐 May–late fall 🚌 26
• On Lake Washington/Portage Bay:
UW Waterfront Activities Center: canoes.
Stadium at east end of car-park.
✉ Waterfront Activities Building ☎ 206/543–9433
🚌 25, 43
• On Lake Union:
Center for Wooden Boats: sailboats and
rowboats.
🚼 B3 ✉ 1010 Valley St ☎ 206/382–2628 🚌 26,
28
Moss Bay Rowing and Kayak Center:
kayaks and shells—lessons, tours, rentals.
🚼 C4 ✉ 1001 Fairview Avenue N #1900
☎ 206/682–2031 🚌 70, 71, 72, 73
Northwest Marine Charters, 26 feet and up,
sails and power; and one-day skippered
outings.
🚼 B3 ✉ 2400 Westlake N ☎ 206/283–3040 🚌 26,
28
NW Outdoor Center: kayaks
🚼 B3 ✉ 1500 Westlake Avenue N ☎ 206/281–9694
🚌 26, 28

FISHING
• A Spot Tail Salmon Guide: Salmon fishing in Puget
Sound with guide and gear provided.
✉ 2318 Viewmont Way W ☎ 206/283–6680 🚌 17
• Seacrest Boat House: aluminum boat rentals with
motor, and bait, half or full day.
🚼 F1 ✉ 1660 Harbor SW ☎ 206/932–1050 🚌 37

GOLF
Seattle has three 18-hole public golf courses and
three practice ranges within the city limits. Tee times
begin between 5 and 6AM, depending on the season.
• Jackson Park
🚼 K3 ✉ NE 135th and 10th Avenue NE, off I-5 ☎ 206/363–4747
🚌 73
• Jefferson Park
🚼 G4 ✉ 4101 Beacon Avenue S ☎ 206/762–9949 🚌 36
• West Seattle Golf Course
🚼 L2 ✉ 4470 35th SW ☎ 206/935–5187 🚌 54, 55
• Green Lake Pitch & Putt is another option. It's a
nine-hole, par three practice course. Iron and putter
rental available.
🚼 A6 ✉ 5701 E Green Lake Way ☎ 206/632–2280 🚌 16

Canoeing on Lake Union

The Burke-Gilman Trail: Highlights
● Fremont neighborhood
● Gasworks Park
● University of Washington campus
● University Village
● Sound Garden public art (nearby)
● Matthews Beach (extension to Sammamish River Trail)
● Woodinville Wineries
● Redhook Brewery, Woodinville

FREE & NEARLY FREE ATTRACTIONS

Free admission days

Many of Seattle's museums and other attractions have free or cheap admission days once a month. Here's a selection:

- First Tuesday of the month: Nordic Heritage Museum; the Children's Museum ("pay as you can" 5–8 PM)

- First Thursday of the month: Seattle Art Museum; Seattle Asian Art Museum

- First Thursday of the month, 5–8PM: Pioneer Square Gallery Walk; Museum of Flight

- Every Thursday: Henry Art Gallery (5–8PM)

- First Saturday of the month: Seattle Asian Art Museum

Seattle Asian Art Museum

58

See Top 25 Sights for
THE BOEING TOUR (► 48)
DISCOVERY PARK & DAYBREAK STAR ART CENTER (► 24)
FERRY TO BAINBRIDGE ISLAND (► 34)
FISHERMEN'S TERMINAL (► 27)
KLONDIKE GOLD RUSH NATIONAL HISTORIC PARK(► 39)
THE HIRAM M. CHITTENDEN LOCKS (► 26)
PIKE PLACE MARKET (► 33)
REI (► 40)
VOLUNTEER PARK (► 42)

GLASS-BLOWING DEMONSTRATIONS
• Denny Park Glass Studio: This full-sized glass-blowing studio and showroom downtown is open to the public weekdays. Tours available.
🕀 D3 ⊠ 818 John Street ☎ 206/343–5995 for reservations 🕔 9–5 🚌 17, 26, 28
• Edge of Glass Gallery: Here at his studio and shop in Fremont, John Walsh creates glass art.
🕀 A3 ⊠ 513 N 36th Street #H ☎ 206/547–6551 🕔 Wed–Sun 11–6 🚌 26, 28
• Glasshouse Art Glass, Ltd: Watch glass-blowers at work in this Pioneer Square studio to the large gallery.
🕀 G6 ⊠ 311 Occidental Avenue S ☎ 206/682–9939 🕔 Mon–Sat 10–3, Sun 11–3 🚌 Any buses on 1st (free zone)

LAKE VIEW CEMETERY
Seattle's pioneers are buried here, but it's the graves of martial arts cult star Bruce Lee (near the top of the hill) and his son, Brandon, that draw visitors.
🕀 C4, C5 ⊠ 1554 15th Ave East at E Garfield on Capitol Hill 🚌 10

BLUEPRINTS: 100 YEARS OF SEATTLE ARCHITECTURE
Interesting free exhibit put together for the Centennial by the Museum of History and Industry.
🕀 B5 ⊠ 3rd floor Atrium, Rainier Square at 5th and University

VOLUNTEER PARK WATER TOWER
Best free view of the city.
🕀 C4, C5 ⊠ West of 15th Ave E between E Prospect and E Galer 🚌 10

YE OLDE CURIOSITY SHOP
This curio and collectibles shop, owned by the same family since it opened in 1899, is best known as the home of Sylvester the mummy.
🕀 G5 ⊠ Pier 54, 1001 Alaskan Way ☎ 206/682–5844 🚌 Waterfront Streetcar

FREE EVENTS

BREWERY TOURS
• Rainier Brewing Company: The grandaddy of local breweries with free tours and tasting.

🔲 G4 ✉ 3100 Airport Way S (south just off I-5) ☎ 206/622–2600 🕐 Mon–Sat 1–6 🚌 130 local

• Pike Place Brewery has a microbrew museum. Tours available.

🔲 F5 ✉ 1415 1st Avenue ☎ 206/622–3373 🕐 11–11 🚌 Downtown free zone

• Pyramid Breweries. Daily tours, with samples of Pyramid Ales and Thomas Kemper lagers and sodas.

🔲 A5 ✉ 1201 1st Avenue S ☎ 206/682–3377 🚌 Downtown free zone

• Redhook Ale Brewery: The first in Seattle with craft brews. Daily tours at two locations, one in Fremont and the other at Woodinville, 25 minutes northeast of Seattle.

✉ 3400 Phinney Avenue N ☎ 206/548–8000 🚌 26, 28
✉ Woodinville ☎ 425/483-3232

ELLIOTT BAY BOOK COMPANY READINGS
This first-rate independent bookstore, great to browse, has a café and a program of readings by noted authors six days a week, usually for free. Arrive early.

🔲 G6 ✉ 101 S Main Street ☎ 206/624–6600 for ticket information 🚌 Downtown free zone

FRYE MUSEUM CONCERTS
Classical music concerts on Sunday afternoons.

🔲 E4 ✉ 704 Terry Ave ☎ 206/622–9250 🚌 3, 4, 12

OUT TO LUNCH WEEKDAY CONCERTS
Midday concerts in summer at various downtown locations. Weekdays, June–September.

☎ 206/623–0340 for information.

UNIVERSITY DISTRICT FARMERS' MARKET
Flowers and farm fresh produce, summer Saturdays.

🔲 A6 ✉ University Way NE and NE 50th 🚌 70, 71, 72, 73, 43

WINERIES
• Chateau Ste. Michelle offers tours and tastings 10–4.30 daily, picnicking on the grounds and summer concerts.

🔲 K3 ✉ 14111 NE 145th Street in Woodinville, 25 minutes NE of Seattle ☎ 425/488–3300

• Columbia Winery: One of Washington's pioneer wineries.

✉ 14030 NE 145th ☎ 425/488–2776

• Bainbridge Island Winery: A small family vineyard and winery. Tastings and picnic area. One-half mile north of the ferry dock on Bainbridge Island.

✉ 682 Hwy 305 ☎ 206/842–WINE 🚌 66 to ferrydock

Hande-made brews

Seattles brewers have pioneered the U.S.'s move away from mass-produced beers to more subtly flavored "craft brews." With at least eight brewpubs in the area, some call Seattle "the microbrew capital of the world."

ATTRACTIONS FOR CHILDREN

Cooling off Seattle-style

A great place for kids

In the 1980's, Seattle launched a major effort to create a more "child-friendly" urban environment that would discourage the exodus of middle class families to the suburbs. The city joined forces with civic groups to create an abundance of outdoor recreation and entertainment venues.

See Top 25 Sights for
BURKE MUSEUM (► 46)
FERRY TO BAINBRIDGE ISLAND (► 34)
LAKE UNION (► 37)
MUSEUM OF FLIGHT (► 43)
PACIFIC SCIENCE CENTER (► 29)
REI (► 40)
THE WATERFRONT & AQUARIUM (► 32)
WOODLAND PARK ZOO (► 28)

CHILDREN'S MUSEUM
Activities focus on the arts and humanities. Children can write their own cartoons and then watch their characters spring to life; build fanciful crafts in artist-led workshops; and enter the time tunnel to ancient Greece.
➕ D2 ✉ The Center House, first level, Seattle Center ☎ 206/441–1768 ⏰ Mon–Fri 10–5 and Sat–Sun 10–6;. Jun–Sep Mon–Fri 10–6; Sat–Sun 10–7. Closed holidays 🚌 3, 4, 6, 16, 24 to Seattle Center

FUN FOREST AMUSEMENT PARK
Rides, carnival games, and cotton candy.
➕ D3 ✉ Seattle Center ☎ 206/728–1585 ⏰ Jun–Aug noon–11. Off season hours vary 🚌 3, 4, 16 to Seattle Center

IMAX
Acclaimed documentaries on giant screens in two theaters.
OMNIDOME: ➕ F5 ✉ Seattle Aquarium 🚌 24, 33
IMAX: ➕ D2 ✉ Pacific Science Center 🚌 3, 4, 5, 24, 33 to Seattle Center

ODYSSEY MARITIME DISCOVERY CENTER
Three state-of-the-art exhibits highlight the working waterfront: you can board a "virtual kayak" and negotiate the Puget Sound inlets, while Harvesting the Sea gives you the opportunity to skipper a commercial fishing boat, and the Ocean Trade gallery allows you to load a container vessel and measure yourself against the pros.
➕ D3 ✉ Bell Harbor's Pier 66 ☎ 206/374–4000 🚌 24, 33; Waterfront streetcar

SEATTLE CHILDREN'S THEATER
Recognized worldwide for its innovative programming. With over 20 seasons under its belt and the fanciful new Charlotte Martin Theater, SCT is a prized cultural resource for families.
➕ D2 ✉ Seattle Center ☎ 206/441–3322 ⏰ Season Sep–Jun 🚌 16, 24, 33 to Seattle Center

SEATTLE
where to...

NORTHWEST/AMERICAN CUISINE

Prices

Average meal per head including tips, excluding drinks:

$ = Under $10

$$ = $10 to $25

$$$ = over $25

CHEZ SHEA (IN THE MARKET) ($$$)

Northwest foods prepared using French techniques in an intimate Pike Place Market hideaway. Smoking permitted in lounge.
🔆 F5 ✉ 94 Pike Street
☎ 206/ 467–9990
🕐 Tue–Sun 5:30–10:30

COASTAL KITCHEN ($$)

Savoury food from the coast—any coast—from fried green tomatoes and Creole crabcakes to Mediterranean salads. Breakfasts, too.
🔆 C5 ✉ 429 15th Avenue E
☎ 206/322–1145 🕐 Daily: breakfast, lunch, dinner 🚌 10

CUTTER'S BAYHOUSE ($$)

Stylish bistro at Pike Place Market with spectacular views, market-fresh food.
🔆 F5 ✉ 2001 Western Avenue ☎ 206/448–4884
🕐 11AM– 1:30AM

FULLERS ($$$)

Celebrity chef Monique Barbeau presides over the kitchen in this polished dining room in the Sheraton Seattle. Reservations recommended.
🔆 E6 ✉ 1400 6th Avenue
☎ 206/ 621–9000 or 206/447–5544 🕐 Mon–Sat; dinner only Sat

GUIDO'S ($)

Dynamite pizza, in two locations.
🔆 A6 ✉ 2108 NE 65th #7900
☎ 206/525–3042 🔆 A6
✉ E Green Lake Drive N,#105
☎ 206/522–5553 🚌 48

KASPAR'S ($$)

Europe -trained chef Kaspar himself grows the herbs used in the contemporary Northwest fare served in this splendid establishment.
🔆 D2 ✉ 19 West Harrison
☎ 206/298–0123 🕐 Dinner only; closed Sun–Mon 🚌 1, 2, 13

METROPOLITAN GRILL ($$$)

A top steakhouse full of wood, brass and leather. Full bar with superb (and remarkably inexpensive) hors d'oeuvres served during happy hour.
🔆 F6 ✉ 820 Second Avenue
🕐 Daily; no lunch weekends
☎ 206/624–3287

OLD SPAGHETTI FACTORY ($$)

This restaurant caters to families and tourists.
🔆 D2 ✉ 2801 Elliott Avenue, near Pier 70 ☎ 206/441–7724
🚋 Waterfront Streetcar (Pier 70)

PAINTED TABLE ($$$)

Superb new American cuisine, beautifully presented in an artful setting.
🔆 F5 ✉ 92 Madison
☎ 206/624–3646
🕐 Breakfast and dinner daily; lunch Mon–Fri

PALACE KITCHEN ($$–$$$)

Culinary heavyweight Tom Douglas's most recent creation serves up delicious Northwest cuisine in a warm, friendly, retro setting. The numerous appetizers and desserts make for great informal dining.

✚ E5 ✉ 2030 5th Avenue
☎ 206/448–2001 🕐 Dinner
only

PALISADE ($$$)

A lavish place with an
interior waterfall and a
fish-filled pool spanned
by a footbridge. The
menu offers a huge
range of fish, meat,
poultry and market-fresh
accompaniments. Great
for Sunday brunch.
✚ D2 ✉ 2601 W Marina
Place (Elliott Bay Marina)
☎ 206/285–1000 🕐 Daily
🚌 19, 24

PEGASUS PIZZA & PASTA ($)

Great views, friendly
staff and Greek-style
pizza that some consider
Seattle's best.
✚ L2 ✉ 2758 Alki Avenue
SW ☎ 206/932–4849
🚌 25

PIZZA PAGLIACCI ($)

A Seattle favorite for
distinctive pizza; call for
whole pizza delivery
(☎ 206/726–1717). Beer
and wine.
✚ A5 ✉ 4529 University
Way NE ☎ 206/632–0421
🚌 71, 72, 73, 43
✚ D4 ✉ 426 Broadway E
☎ 206/324–0730 🚌 7
Queen Anne
✚ C2 ✉ 550 Queen Anne
Avenue N ☎ 206/285–1232
🚌 13

RED ROBIN ($–$$)

Overlooks Portage Bay.
Great burgers, salads
and, fajitas. Noisy but
very child-friendly.
✚ A4 ✉ Ten locations. The
original is at 3272 Fuhrman Avenue
E, just south of University Bridge
🚌 25

SIX DEGREES ($–$$)

Wildly popular
neighborhood kitchen
with delicious noshes like
burgers, ribs and baked
beans. Upbeat and fun.
✚ L3 ✉ 7900 Green Lake
Drive N ☎ 206/523–1600
🕐 Mon–Fri 11–10; Sat–Sun
11–midnight 🚌 16, 2

THEOZ RESTAURANT & BAR ($$)

Acclaimed chef Emily
Moore's newest downtown
establishment features a
signature crusty beef and
grilled porterhouse steak,
and original offerings like
smoke-roasted duck with
zinfandel-chipotle jus.
✚ F6 ✉ 1523 6th Avenue
☎ 206/749–9660 🕐 Closed
Sat–Sun lunch

WOLFGANG PUCK CAFÉ ($)

Trendy informal eatery
next to the Harbor Steps;
a branch of the California
original with the same
tasty wood-fired pizzas, as
well as sandwiches,
appetizers and salads.
✚ F5 ✉ 1221 1st Avenue
☎ 206/621–9653

Common meals café ($)

This non-profit restaurant serves
delicious, hearty meals at budget
prices while training homeless
men and women for jobs in the
food service industry. The
weekday lunch buffet, which
includes a range of remarkably
ambitious preparations, is popular
and on Thursday nights, top chefs
from local restaurants prepare
outstanding dinners. There's a
fixed price for full-course meals
and all proceeds are plowed back
into the program.
✚ E5 ✉ 1902 2nd Avenue
🕐 Lunch Mon–Fri 11–2, dinner
Thu only ☎ 206/439–5361

SEAFOOD & VEGETARIAN

Anthony's Homeport Restaurants ($$)

Airy and attractive waterfront restaurants each afford fine waterfront views and fresh seafood, salads, and desserts. Full bar.

✚ D3 ✉ Pier 66, 2201 Alaskan Way, on the waterfront
☎ 206/448–6688
🚃 Waterfront trolley
✚ G1 ✉ At Shilshloe in Ballard, 6135 Seaview NW
☎ 206/783–0780 🚌 46

SEAFOOD

BELL STREET DINER ($)

Open daily for lunch and dinner; informal, lower-priced eatery downstairs from Anthony's serves innovative combinations like Manila clam chili, and mahi mahi tacos plus delicious, original desserts.
✚ D3 ✉ Bell St Pier 66, 2201 Alaskan Way
☎ 206/448–6688 🕐 Daily
🚃 Waterfront trolley

BROOKLYN SEAFOOD, STEAK & OYSTER HOUSE ($$)

Great oyster bar; first-rate seafood and steak. Wheelchair access.
✚ F5 ✉ 1212 2nd Avenue (across from Seattle Art Museum)
☎ 206/224–7000
🕐 Mon–Fri 11–10; Sat–Sun 4:30–10

CHANDLER'S CRABHOUSE ($$$)

If you love crab, this is the place. On Lake Union with a terrace that's open in good weather.
✚ C4 ✉ 901 Fairview N
☎ 206/223–2722 🕐 lunch and dinner 🚌 71, 72, 73

CHINOOK'S AT SALMON BAY ($$)

Seafood fresh off the boat. Breakfast, too, at weekends.
✚ L2 ✉ 1900 W Nickerson St
☎ 206/283–4665 🕐 lunch and dinner 🚌 19, 24

DUKE'S CHOWDERHOUSE ($-$$)

Excellent clam chowder and seafood at budget prices. Outdoor seating in good weather. Very popular.
✚ L2 ✉ 7850 Green Lake Drive N ☎ 206/522–4908
🚌 16, 26
✚ C4 ✉ 901 Fairview N on Chandler's Cove, Lake Union
☎ 206/382–9963 🕐 Lunch and dinner 🚌 71, 72, 73

ETTA'S SEAFOOD ($$$)

Award-winning chef Tom Douglas's '90s-style seafood house at the Market features an extensive and innovative menu.
✚ E5 ✉ 2020 Western Avenue 🕐 Lunch and dinner
☎ 206/443–6000

FLYING FISH ($$-$$$)

This swanky, hip, and, often noisy Belltown eatery serves both Northwest seafood and exotic imports. Go with friends for a seafood orgy and order "platters by the pound "
✚ E5 ✉ 2234 1st Avenue
☎ 206/728–8595 🕐 Dinner only

IVAR'S SALMON HOUSE (££)

This Northwest institution on Lake Union's north shore is well known for its smoked salmon, clam chowder and cornbread. Full bar. Also, fish bar with informal outdoor seating. Sunday brunch.
✚ A4 ✉ 401 NE Northlake Way 🕐 Daily 🚌 26

PESCATORE (££)

Feast on fresh wild salmon as you watch boats work their way through the ship canal. Breezy and fashionable, at Hiram M Chittenden Locks.

🏠 G1 ✉ 5300 34th NW
☎ 206/784–1733 🕐 Daily

PONTI SEAFOOD GRILL (£££)

Seafood with an ethnic flair—notably black pepper tuna carpaccio and Thai curry penne with scallops and crabmeat. Outdoor dining in summer. Sunday brunch. Next to the Fremont Bridge.

🏠 B2 ✉ 3014 3rd Avenue N
☎ 206/284–3000 🕐 Daily
🚍 26

RAY'S BOATHOUSE (£££)

Superior seafood to order as well as excellent service, and a fine wine list, plus a waterfront view of Shilshloe Marina.

🏠 G1 ✉ 6049 Seaview Avenue NW ☎ 206/789–3770
🕐 Daily 🚍 46

SALTY'S ON ALKI (££–£££)

Fresh seafood in an engaging setting with outdoor seating and a smashing view of downtown across Elliott Bay. Sunday brunch 9–1:30.

🏠 L2 ✉ 1936 Harbor SW
☎ 206/937–1600 🕐 Daily; lunch and dinner 🚍 37

SHUCKERS (IN THE FOUR SEASONS OLYMPIC HOTEL) (££)

Superb seafood— whole crab, salmon, and geoduck stew. For oysters, this is *the* place.

🏠 F6 ✉ 411 University Street
☎ 206/621–1984 🕐 Closed Sun lunch 🚍 17, 46

STEAMERS SEAFOOD CAFÉ (£)

Fresh fish bar, three locations. Beer and wine.

🏠 F5 ✉ Pier 56, 1200 Alaskan Way
☎ 206/623–2066
🚃 Waterfront trolley
🏠 F5 ✉ Pier 59, 1500 Alaskan Way
☎ 206/624–0312
🏠 D3 ✉ 313 Harrison
☎ 206/728–2228 🚍 3, 4, 6, 16

VEGETARIAN

CAFÉ FLORA (££)

Imaginative seasonal vegetarian menu and a stylish, sophisticated setting. Patio. Weekend brunch.

🏠 C6 ✉ 2901 E Madison St
☎ 206/325–9100 🕐 Closed Mon 🚍 11

GRAVITY BAR (£)

This futuristic space straight out of the bar in *Return of the Jedi* features a signature "wheatgrass" juice among its huge selection of juices.

🏠 D4 ✉ 415 Broadway E in the Broadway Market
☎ 206/325–7186 🕐 Daily
🚍 7

ASIAN CUISINE

Sushi

Sanmi Sushi ($$)

This tiny, unassuming eatery next to Palisades on Magnolia's Smith Cove has, some say, the best sushi in town. Beer, wine, sake.
✚ D2 ✉ 2601 Marina Place ☎ 206/283–9978 ⏰ Closed Sat–Sun lunch 🚌 19, 24

BAHN THAI ($$)

Delicious Thai specialties in an ornate setting replete with gilded statuary. A short walk from Seattle Center on lower Queen Anne.
✚ C3 ✉ 409 Roy ☎ 206/283–0444 ⏰ No lunch weekends 🚌 15, 18, 1, 2, 13

BLOWFISH ASIAN CAFE ($$)

Cutting edge styling and delicious pan-Asian cuisine at affordable prices downtown in the Paramount Hotel. Open daily for breakfast, lunch and dinner.
✚ E6 ✉ 722 Pine Street ☎ 206/467–7777 ⏰ Daily

BUSH GARDEN ($$)

A huge, lavish restaurant that's an insitution in the International District. Extensive menu, tatami rooms, karaoke.
✚ E4 ✉ 614 Maynard Avenue S ☎ 206/682–6830 ⏰ Closed Sun lunch 🚌 1, 7, 15

CHUTNEY'S GRILLE ON THE HILL ($–$$)

Classic Indian cooking stars in this attractive bistro on Capitol Hill.
✚ C5 ✉ 605 15th Avenue E ☎ 206/726–1000 ⏰ Closed Sun lunch 🚌 10

FREMONT NOODLE HOUSE ($)

Steaming rice-noodle soups come with sprouts, mint, lime, and chili sauce on the side to add as you wish. Order the Thai appetizer tray to sample all the flavors. Beer and wine only.
✚ A3 ✉ 3411 Fremont Avenue N ☎ 206/547–1550 ⏰ Closed Mon 🚌 26

NHK MALAYSIAN RESTAURANT ($)

This no-frills eatery in a strip mall in Little Saigon serves authentic Malaysian food. Signature dishes include soft flatbread (roti canai) and beef and chicken satays. No alcohol.
✚ E4 ✉ 212 12th Avenue S ☎ 206/324–4091 ⏰ Daily

NIKKO (AT THE WESTIN HOTEL) ($$$)

Elegant Japanese cuisine from sushi to steak. Complimentary hors d'oeuvres in bar 5–7. Private tatami rooms available.
✚ E5 ✉ 1900 Fifth Avenue ☎ 206/322–4641 ⏰ Mon–Fri lunch; Mon–Sat dinner

NOODLE RANCH ($)

Innovative design meets fine Pan-Asian cuisine in this Belltown haunt opened by two artists and their Southeast Asian chef.
✚ E5 ✉ 2228 2nd Avenue ☎ 206/728–0463 ⏰ Closed Sun

WILD GINGER RESTAURANT & SATAY BAR ($$–$$$)

Critically acclaimed Pan-Asian restaurant west of Pike Place Market.
✚ E3 ✉ 1400 Western Avenue (below Pike Place Market) ☎ 206/ 623–4450 ⏰ Closed Sun lunch

ITALIAN/MEDITERRANEAN

ADRIATICA ($$$)

Two flights of stairs take you to some great Mediterranean food. Delectable from the first bites of fried calamari to your last of chocolate espresso soufflé.

➕ C3 ✉ 1107 Dexter Avenue N ☎ 206/285–5000 🕓 Dinner only

AL BOCCALINO ($$–$$$)

Rustic Pioneer Square eatery with lots of stained glass, dark wood, and brick walls. Go for the innovative antipasti, succulent seafood, or order the aged porterhouse steak. Daily specials.

➕ G6 ✉ 1 Yesler Way ☎ 206/622–7688 🕓 Closed Sat–Sun lunch

ANDALUCA($$)

Fine mediterranean flavors in a romantic room in the Mayflower Park Hotel. Note the menu of "small plates and shareables.", tapas (5–6:30), great martinis, and adventurous wine selection. Reservations recommended.

➕ E5 ✉ 407 Olive Way at Westlake Center ☎ 206/382–6999 🕓 Closed Sun lunch

BUCA DI BEPPO ($$)

Congenial family restaurant where you'll find large platters of southern Italian food to share, so go with a group. You'll swear you're in Little Italy—a shrine to Italian kitsch.

➕ D3 ✉ 701 9th Avenue N ☎ 206/ 244–2288 🚌 26, 28

THE PINK DOOR ($$)

A delightful place for hearty Italian food in a funky trattoria setting. Outdoor seating in warm weather.

➕ F5 ✉ 1919 Post Alley ☎ 206/443–3241 🕓 Closed Sun–Mon

SOSTANZA ($$)

You could well be in Tuscany, sipping wine and dining on choice regional specialties, in this warm Madison Park establishment. Lunch is à la carte; dinner, a three-course prix fixe meal. Beer and wine only. Good value.

➕ A2 ✉ 1927 43rd Ave E ☎ 206/ 324–9701 🕓 Closed Sat lunch and all Sun

TULIO ($$)

Situated in the Vintage Park Hotel this award winning establishment is a favorite with many Seattleites.

➕ F6 ✉ 1100 5th Avenue ☎ 206/624–5500 🕓 Daily

TRATTORIA MITCHELLI ($–$$)

Pasta and pizza at reasonable prices in Pioneer Square haunt. Noisy. Open early to late.

➕ G6 ✉ 84 Yesler ☎ 206/623–3883 🕓 Daily till late

BEST OF THE REST

CONTINENTAL

CAFÉ CAMPAGNE ($$)
Tiny French bistro in the Market. Beer and wine only.
➕ F5 ✉ 1600 Post Alley ☎ 206/728–2233 ⊕ Closed Sun dinner

CAMPAGNE ($$$)
Celebrated French country cuisine served on crisp white linen. Smoking in the lounge.
➕ F5 ✉ 86 Pine Street at Market ☎ 206/728–2800 ⊕ Daily

DU JOUR ($)
European cuisine featuring fresh salads, baked goods and soups in pleasant surroundings near the market.
➕ F5 ✉ 1919 1st Avenue ☎ 206/441–3354 ⊕ Daily

ROVER'S ($$$)
French cuisine in an elegant, romantic, Madison Valley setting Patio seating in warm weather. Fine wine selection.
➕ C6 ✉ 2808 E. Madison ☎ 206/ 325–7442 ⊕ Closed Sun–Mon 🚌 11

SZMANIA'S ($$–$$$)
Stylish Magnolia restaurant opened by the former head chef of the Four Seasons Olympic Hotel. Refined take on German specialties.
➕ E6 ✉ 3321 W McGraw St ☎ 206/ 284–7305 🚌 19, 24

VIRAZON ($$$)
Wild game and local seafood are artfully prepared with French flair in this tiny gem of a restaurant. Lovely European ambience. Near Seattle Art Museum and Pike Place Market.
➕ F5 ✉ 1329 1st Avenue and Union ☎ 206/233–0123

MEXICAN/SOUTH-WEST

AZTECA ($)
Family-friendly chain with hearty Mexican cooking; multiple locations.
➕ B4 ✉ 2501 Fairview E on Lake Union ☎ 206/324–4941
➕ A6 ✉ 2686 University Village Mall ☎ 206/524–2987
🚌 70, 71, 72, 73

CACTUS ($$)
Southwest cuisine; upbeat family-friendly setting.
➕ B6 ✉ 4220 E Madison ☎ 206/324–4140 ⊕ Closed Sun lunch 🚌 11

MAMA'S MEXICAN KITCHEN ($)
A funky, lively, and affordable, Belltown institution that serves up hearty portions of tasty Mexican food. Outdoor seating in good weather.
➕ E5 ✉ 2234 2nd Avenue ☎ 206/ 728–6262 ⊕ Daily

COFFEE, TEA, & LIGHT FARE

B & O ESPRESSO ($)
Famous for desserts and coffee. The original Capitol Hill coffeehouse is intimate and elegant.
🏢 D4 ✉ 204 Belmont Avenue E ☎ 206/322–5028 🚌 43
🏢 D4 ✉ 401 Broadway E ☎ 206/328–3290 🚌 7
🏢 G6 ✉ 103 Cherry Street ☎ 206/621–9372 🕐 Closed Sun

CAFÉ DILETTANTE
Crowded café with mirrored walls attracts chocolate lovers. Chose the Coupe Dilettante, an ice cream sundae with a signiture dark chocolate Ephemere sauce.
🏢 D4 ✉ 416 Broadway E ☎ 206/329–6463 🕐 Daily

CAFÉ NOLA ($)
Small café owned by two sisters (one of them restaurateur Wolgang Pucks's former pastry chef). Baked goods, baguettes, soups, and salads.
🏢 L1 ✉ 101 Winslow Way E, Bainbridge Island ☎ 206/842–3822 🕐 Closed dinner and Mon 🚌 66 to ferry

QUEEN MARY TEAHOUSE ($$$)
High tea served every day in the British tradition, with scrumptious baked goods. Breakfast and lunch too.
🏢 A6 ✉ 2912 NE 55th Street, University District ☎ 206/527–2770 🕐 Daily

STILL LIFE IN FREMONT ($)
This popular neighborhood eatery resembling a "beat" coffeehouse from the 1950s, offers up tasty soups, salads, sandwiches, and acoustic entertainment in the evenings.
🏢 A3 ✉ 709 N 35th Street ☎ 206/547–9850 🕐 Daily 🚌 26

TEAHOUSE KUAN YIN ($)
Seattle's first teahouse with a full selection of teas and multicultural choice of snacks and desserts.
🏢 A3 ✉ 1911 N. 45th Street in Wallingford ☎ 206/632–2055 🕐 Daily 🚌 16

TORREFAZIONE ITALIA
Smooth, flavorful espresso drinks served in Italian hand-painted pottery. A Tuscan experience.
🏢 F6 ✉ 1310 4th Ave ☎ 206/583–8970 🕐 Closed Sun
🏢 E6 ✉ 622 Olive Way, Downtown ☎ 206/624–1429 🕐 Closed Sun
🏢 G6 ✉ 320 Occidental Avenue, Pioneer Square ☎ 206/624–5847

VIVACE
Come here for some of the best espresso drinks around town. Sidewalk viewing on Broadway.
🏢 D4 ✉ 321 Broadway Avenue E 🚌 7

ZIO RICCO
Elegant European ambience in this downtown café. Espresso, sandwiches, salads, juice bar, desserts.
🏢 E5 ✉ 1415 4th Avenue ☎ 206/467–8616 🕐 Closed evenings and all Sun

Bagels

Bagel Oasis ($)
Delicious bagels with a variety of spreads. Several locations including:
Fremont 🏢 A2 ✉ 462 N 36th 🚌 26, 28
Downtown 🏢 F6 ✉ 4th and Seneca 🕐 Closed dinner

Seattle Bagel Bakery ($)
First-rate bagels. Order "to go" for a picnic outside, on the Harbor Steps.
🏢 F5 ✉ 1302 Western Avenue ☎ 206/624–2187

MEN'S & WOMEN'S CLOTHING

Shopping districts

Seattle's finest clothing shops tend to be clustered in several neighborhoods: City Center around 5th and Pike; 1st Avenue on the southern edge of Belltown (primarily women's clothing); along Broadway E on Capitol Hill and University Village at NE 45th Street and 25th Avenue NE (women's apparel).

CASUAL WEAR/ OUTDOOR APPAREL

BANANA REPUBLIC
Casual clothes in natural fibers.
🕂 E6 ✉ 500 Pike Street in Coliseum Bldg
☎ 206/622–2303

EDDIE BAUER
Casual wear and accessories for men and women with an outdoor lifestyle.
🕂 F6 ✉ 1330 5th Avenue across from Rainier Square
☎ 206/622–2766
🕔 Mon–Fri 10–8; Sat 10–7, Sun 11–6

THE NORTH FACE
Hiking and climbing gear, sportswear for the outdoors; skiwear.
🕂 F6 ✉ 1023 1st Avenue
☎ 206/622–4111

PATAGONIA
State of the art outdoor clothing for adults and children.
🕂 E5 ✉ 2100 1st Avenue
☎ 206/ 622–9700

REI
Outdoor clothing and gear runs the gamut from hiking equipment to bikes, kayaks, and nature books.
🕂 D4 ✉ 222 Yale Avenue N
☎ 206/223–1944

WARSHAL'S
Sporting goods emporium of the "Army & Navy Store" genre with a large selection of hunting, fishing, and camping equipment, plus outdoor clothing, boots, and a photo department.
🕂 F6 ✉ 1000 1st Avenue
☎ 206/624–7300 🕔 Closed Sun

FASHION (BY NEIGHBORHOOD)

DOWNTOWN CITY CENTER

BARNEYS
Chic and trendy for that minimalist New York style. Prada and other popular designers. Shoes, jewelry, accessories, and skin products.
🕂 F6 ✉ 1420 5th Avenue in City Center ☎ 206/622–6300

BETSEY JOHNSON
For adventuresome and young-at-heart women who expect a bit of fun and flamboyance in their clothing.
🕂 F6 ✉ 1429 5th Avenue
☎ 206/624–2887

BROOKS BROTHERS
Superior men's clothing in traditional styles.
🕂 F6 ✉ 1335 5th Avenue
☎ 206/624–4400

BURBERRY'S
Tailored clothing and accessories in the British style including the famous trench coat.
🕂 E6 ✉ 409 Pike Street
☎ 206/621–2000

BUTCH BLUM
Expensive European-styled men's apparel from famous designers' exclusive collections, as well as more original, avant-garde lines.
🕂 F6 ✉ 1408 5th Avenue
☎ 206/622–5760 🕔 Closed Sun

HELEN'S (OF COURSE)

Exclusive fashions for women over 50 with haute couture from Oscar de la Renta and other designers.

✚ F6 ✉ 1302 5th Avenue ☎ 206/624–4000 ⏱ Closed Sun

MARIO'S

Fashionable downtown clothing store specializing in clean, classic lines and featuring designers like Donna Karan and Giorgio Armani. Also shoes and accessories.

✚ E6 ✉ 1513 6th Avenue ☎ 206/ 223–1461

NORDSTROM

The flagship store downtown stocks clothing for the entire family including designer wear. Noted nationwide for its excellent service.

✚ E5 ✉ 1601 2nd Avenue ☎ 206/628–2111

NUBIAS

Relaxed sophistication for women in styles that reflect owner-designer Nubia's Latin roots with accents from Asia.

✚ E6 ✉ 1507 6th Avenue and 4116 E Madison in Madison Park ☎ 206/622 0297 🚌 11

TOTALLY MICHAEL'S

Sophisticated women's clothing for work, play and after dark.

✚ F6 ✉ 521 Union Street ☎ 206/622–4920 ⏱ Closed Sun

BELLTOWN (ALONG 1ST AVENUE)

BABY & CO.

Pricey, whimsical clothes for adventurous women.

✚ E5 ✉ 1936 1st Avenue ☎ 206/448–4077

C.P. SHADES

Casually sophisticated natural fiber women's clothing—dresses, pants, skirts, vests, and tunics made of cotton, silky rayon, and velvet; deep, subtle hues.

✚ E5 ✉ 2025 1st Avenue #A ☎ 206/448–9218

DAKOTA

Classic women's clothes and accessories by American designers.

✚ E5 ✉ 2025 1st Avenue ☎ 206/441–3177

DARBURY STENDERU

Stunning wearable art for women with hand-painted designs; beautiful colors and fabrics.

✚ E5 ✉ 2121 1st Avenue ☎ 206/448–2625 ⏱ Closed Sun

DITA BOUTIQUE

Unusual selections of women's wear for all ages, including many imports.

✚ F5 ✉ 1525 1st Avenue, #2 ☎ 206/622–1770

ENDLESS KNOT

Elegant and original women's clothes.

✚ E5 ✉ 2232 1st Avenue ☎ 206/448–0355

FAST FORWARD

Cutting edge chic for women.

✚ E5 ✉ 1918 1st Avenue ☎ 206/728–8050

OPUS 204

Custom designed women's clothing, jewelry, and accessories—sophisti- cated, simple lines in

71

Size conversion

A = American
B = British
F = France
I = Italy
E = Rest of Europe

Women's clothes

A	8	10	12	14	16
B	10	12	14	16	18
F	38	40	42	46	48
I	40	42	44	46	48
E	36	38	40	42	44

Men's shirts

A	14½	15	15½	16	16½
B	14½	15	15½	16	16½
E	37	38	39/40	41	42

Shoes

A	5½	6½	7½	8½	9½	10½	11½
B	4	5	6	7	8	9	11
E	36	38	39	40	41	42	44

beautiful fabrics. Antiques and collectibles as well.
➕ E5 ✉ 2004 1st Avenue
☎ 206/728–7707 ▣ 7

CAPITOL HILL (ALONG BROADWAY)

URBAN OUTFITTERS
New and vintage clothing popular with the young and trendy; also housewares, jewelry, gifts. In the Broadway Market.
➕ D4 ✉ 401 Broadway E
☎ 206/322–1800 ▣ 7

YAZDI'S
Dresses, skirts, vests, and softly draping pants for women—made of rayon and cotton in beautiful Indonesian prints.
➕ D4 ✉ 401 Broadway E
☎ 206/860–7109 ▣ 7
Other stores in Pike Place Market and Wallingford Center

PIONEER SQUARE

DESIGN PRODUCTS CLOTHING
Distinctive women's clothing from casual to tailored, including evening wear. Local designer Deliane Klein is well represented.
➕ F3 ✉ 208 1st Avenue S
☎ 206/624–7795

FLYING SHUTTLE
Beautiful hand-woven women's clothing and wearable art; handpainted silk purses and scarves and exquisite jewelry.
➕ G6 ✉ 607 1st Avenue in Pioneer Square
☎ 206/343–9762

UNIVERSITY VILLAGE

ABERCROMBIE & FITCH
Well-made clothes for well-heeled men and women.
➕ A6 ✉ 2540 NE University Village ☎ 206/729–3510

THE GAP
Yes, the Gap. Essential stop for casual coordinates for both men and women.
➕ A6 ✉ 2730 NE University Village Ct. ☎ 206/535–2146
Also at:
☎ 206/523–0450
☎ 206/524–6954

MARLEE
Reasonably priced women's clothes and accessories for work and play, many by local designers.
➕ A6 ✉ 2652 NE University Village Mall ☎ 206/522–6526

ART & ANTIQUES

CLARKE & CLARKE TRIBAL ARTS

Tribal and ethnic antiques and art; notably from Africa, Asia, and the Americas.

🞡 G6 ✉ 524 1st Avenue
☎ 206/447–7017
🕐 Wed–Sat 11–5:30

CRANE GALLERY

Museum quality Asian antiques.

🞡 C2 ✉ 104 W Roy
☎ 206/298–9425 🕐 Closed Sun

FLURY & CO GALLERY

Vintage photographs of Native American life; Native American artifacts, rugs, pottery, beadwork, and carvings.

🞡 F3 ✉ 322 1st Avenue S
☎ 206/587–0260

FOSTER-WHITE GALLERY

Work by Pilchuk Glass artists like Dale Chihuly and prominent artists like Mark Tobey.

🞡 F6 ✉ 1420 5th Avenue, 2nd floor in City Center
☎ 206/340–8025 🞡 G6
✉ 311½ Occidental Avenue S
☎ 206/622–2833

G. GIBSON GALLERY

Photographs and related fine art including works by notable Northwest artists like Marsha Burns.

🞡 G6 ✉ 122 S Jackson, Suite 200 ☎ 206/587–4033
🕐 Tue–Fri 11–5:30, Sat 11–5

GREG KUCHERA GALLERY

One of the city's top galleries.

🞡 G6 ✉ 212 3rd Avenue S
☎ 206/624–0770 🕐 Closed Mon

HONEYCHURCH ANTIQUES

The foremost shop for fine Asian antiques, especially Japanese and Chinese.

🞡 E4 ✉ 1008 James Street
☎ 206/622–1225
🕐 Tue–Sat 11–5

THE LEGACY

Seattle's oldest and finest gallery for Northwest Native American and Inuit art and artifacts. Founded in 1933.

🞡 G6 ✉ 1003 1st Avenue
☎ 206/624–6350, 800/729–1562 🕐 Closed Sun

NORTHWEST GALLERY OF FINE WOODWORKING

Local artists' cooperative that exhibits phenomenal craftsmanship and design.

🞡 G6 ✉ 101 S Jackson
☎ 206/625–0542

STONINGTON GALLERY

Works by native North-west Coast master artists Joe David, Robert Davidson, Bill Holm, and Duane Pasco and by owner/watercolorist Nancy Stonington and others.

🞡 E5 ✉ 2030 1st Avenue
☎ 206/405–4040

WILLIAM TRAVER GALLERY

Contemporary painting, sculpture, and ceramics by major artists. The gallery is also a leading dealer in contemporary studio glass.

🞡 F5 ✉ 110 Union, 2nd floor
☎ 206/587–6501

BOOKS, CD'S & TAPES

The independant bookseller

Seattle has a number of excellent independent booksellers who are committed to bringing quality literature to the public, both blockbusters and smaller works appealing to a more specialized audience. With the arrival of national chains and their well-appointed superstores, independents are feeling the pinch.

BAILEY-COY BOOKS

An inviting, well-stocked bookstore on Capitol Hill with a good selection of gay and lesbian titles.

✚ D4 ✉ 414 Broadway E ☎ 206/323–8842 🚌 7

BUD'S JAZZ RECORDS

Jazz on LP, CD, or video.

✚ G6 ✉ 102 S Jackson in Pioneer Square ☎ 206/628–0445

EAST-WEST BOOKSHOP

One of the region's largest collections of New Age books.

✚ A6 ✉ 1032 NE 65th Street ☎ 206/523–3726 🚌 48

ELLIOTT BAY BOOK COMPANY

More than 130,000 titles, frequent readings, and a café in this Pioneer Square haunt.

✚ G6 ✉ 101 S Main St ☎ 206/624–6600

RED & BLACK BOOKS

This Capitol Hill bookshop gives voice to women writers and cultural and ethnic minorities.

✚ C5 ✉ 432 15th Avenue E ☎ 206/322–7323 🚌 10

SECOND STORY BOOKS

Small shop on the 2nd floor of Wallingford Center with an excellent selection of titles.

✚ Off map at A4 ✉ 1815 N 45th ☎ 206/547–4605 🚌 16

SUB POP MEGA MART

Unassuming hole-in-the-wall from the record label that propelled Seattle into the international limelight. Also posters and grunge memorabilia.

✚ E5 ✉ 1928 2nd Avenue ☎ 206/443–0322

TOWER RECORDS

An awesome variety of music for every taste. A Ticketmaster sells tickets to many concerts and events in the U District store.

✚ A6 ✉ 4321 University Way NE ☎ 206/632–1187 🚌 71, 72, 73, 43

✚ C3 ✉ 500 Mercer near Seattle Center ☎ 206/283–4456 🚌 1, 2, 13

TWICE-SOLD TALES

Wonderful second-hand bookstore.

✚ D4 ✉ 905 E John Street ☎ 206/324–2421 🚌 7, 43

UNIVERSITY BOOKSTORE

One of the nation's largest university bookstores. Also sells art and office supplies, gifts and CDs.

✚ D5 ✉ 4326 University Way NE ☎ 206/634–3400 🚌 71, 72, 73, 43

WIDE WORLD BOOKS & MAPS

Vast array of travel books and a staff of experienced travelers.

✚ Off map at A4 ✉ 1911 N 45th in the Wallingford Center ☎ 206/634–3453 🚌 16

GIFTS

CALDWELL'S
Wonderful imports
including folk art, textiles,
jewelry, and gift items
from Central and South
America, Africa, Asia.
➕ A6 ✉ 2646 University
Village NE ☎ 206/522–7531
🕐 Closed Sun 🚌 25

**CRACKERJACK
CONTEMPORARY
CRAFTS**
Unique handcrafted items
—many by local artists.
➕ Off map at A4 ✉ 1815 N
45th Street (Wallingford Center)
☎ 206/ 547–4983 🚌 16

DESIGN CONCERN
Everything from desk
accessories and
housewares to jewelry,
with one thing in
common: first-rate design.
➕ F6 ✉ 1420 5th Avenue
(City Center)
☎ 206/623–4444

**FIREWORKS FINE
CRAFTS GALLERY**
Where crafts meet art, for
the playful, the beautiful,
and unique. Three
locations:
➕ G6 ✉ 210 1st Avenue S
☎ 206/682–8707
➕ E6 ✉ Westlake Center
☎ 206/682–6462
➕ A6 ✉ University Village
Mall ☎ 206/527–2858

KOBO
Traditional and contem-
porary objects with a
distinctive Japanese flavor.
➕ C3 ✉ 814 E. Roy Street on
Capitol Hill ☎ 206/726–0704.
🕐 Open after noon; closed Mon

**LA TIENDA FOLK ART
GALLERY**
Handcrafted folk art,
textiles, women's apparel,

jewelry, and musical
instruments.
➕ A6 ✉ 4138 University Way
NE ☎ 206/632–1796
🕐 Closed Mon 🚌 71, 72, 73,
43

**MADE IN
WASHINGTON**
Handcrafts, foods and
wines from the region.
Shipping available.
➕ E6 ✉ 400 Pine Street, suite
114, Westlake Center
☎ 206/623–9753
➕ F5 ✉ Pike Place Market
and other locations

**PHOENIX RISING
GALLERY**
Fine crafts gallery in the
north end of the Market
showcasing beautiful and
original jewelry, ceramics,
and glassware.
➕ F5 ✉ 2030 Western
Avenue in the Pike Place Market
☎ 206/728–2332
🕐 Mon–Sat 10–6, Sun 12–5

PORTAGE BAY GOODS
Artisan made,
environmentally friendly
gifts by local and world-
wide artisans.
➕ E6 ✉ 1121 Pike Street
☎ 206/622–3212
🕐 Mon–Fri 11–7, Sat 10–6,
Sun noon–5

SUNDANCE
Robert Redford owns this
chain of "Western rustic"
gifts, furniture, and
accessories.
➕ A6 ✉ 2683 NE University
Village Mall ☎ 206/729–0750
🚌 25 🕐 Closed Sun

SPECIALTY SHOPS

CITY KITES/CITY TOYS
Fun shop on the Pike
Street Hillclimb below the
Market featuring kites and
other flying objects, games
and toys.
✚ E6 ✉ 1501 Western
Avenue ☎ 206/622–5349

**DOWNTOWN HARLEY
DAVIDSON**
The world's largest
collection of Harley
Davidson motorcycling
clothing and collectibles.
✚ E6 ✉ 1912 4th Avenue
☎ 206/448–5661

FACERE JEWELRY ART
One-of-a-kind Victorian
and contemporary jewelry.
✚ F6 ✉ 1420 5th Avenue in
City Center ☎ 206/624–6768

FOX'S GEM SHOP
Fine jewelry since 1912.
Expensive.
✚ F6 ✉ 1341 5th Avenue
☎ 206/623–2528 ✪ Open
Mon–Fri 10–6, Sat 10–5:30

**IMPRESS RUBBER
STAMPS**
Thousands of rubber
stamps, pads, and papers.
✚ E6 ✉ 400 Pine Street in
Westlake Center
☎ 206/621–1878

**LARK IN THE
MORNING**
Beautiful hand-made
musical instruments. In
Pike Place Market.
✚ E5 ✉ 1411 1st Avenue
☎ 206/6623–3440

**THE NATURE
COMPANY**
Everything from fossils
and windchimes to
telescopes and nature
books. Pike Place Market
area.

✚ F5 ✉ 2003 Western
Avenue ☎ 206/6443–1608

THE SHARPER IMAGE
State-of-the-art gadgets.
✚ E6 ✉ 1501 4th Avenue,
Suite 116 ☎ 206/6343–9125
✪ Mon–Sat 10–6, Sun 11–5

TURN OFF THE TV
Unique family-oriented
games and puzzles with an
educational bent.
✚ E6 ✉ 400 Pine Street in
Westlake Center
☎ 206/521–0564

UWAJIMAYA
Largest Asian gift shop
and grocery in the Pacific
Northwest.
✚ E4 ✉ 519 6th Avenue S in
International District ☎ 206/
624–6248. ✪ 9–8 🚌 7, 14,
36

**YE OLDE CURIOSITY
SHOP**
Century-old store/
museum with a fascinating
hodge-podge of North-
west momentos—many
bizarre and grotesque.
✚ G5 ✉ Pier 54 on Alaskan
Way ☎ 206/682–5844

KITSCH, FUNK & RETRO

ARCHIE MCPHEE & CO.
First stop for gag gifts and novelties including plastic cockroaches, inflatable sharks, rubber chickens, and boxing nun puppets.
✚ A3 ✉ 3510 Stone Way N
☎ 206/545–8344 🚌 26

BETSEY JOHNSON
Bright, out-there designer funk: short skirts, spandex and snakeskin corsets.
✚ F6 ✉ 1429 5th Avenue
☎ 206/624–2887

DELUXE JUNK
Vintage clothing, pure kitsch, chic junk, and rattan furniture.
✚ A3 ✉ 3518 Fremont Place
☎ 206/634–2733 🚌 26

GLAMORAMA
Vintage clothes and novelties.
✚ A3 ✉ 3414 Fremont Avenue N ☎ 206/632–0287

ISADORAS
High-end vintage finery: beaded cocktail dresses, vintage gowns and, for men, suits, hats, and ties.
✚ E5 ✉ 1915 First Avenue, 2 blocks north of Market
☎ 206/441–7711

RED LIGHT
Glitzy platform shoes, wigs, retro pants and tops and more.
✚ Off map at A5 ✉ 4560 University Way NE
☎ 206/545–4044 🚌 71, 72, 73, 43

REHEAT
Great fun in this kitchen store with an assortment of vintage and modern kitchenware.
✚ D3 ✉ 2326 2nd Avenue in Belltown ☎ 206/374–0544

RETRO VIVA
Retro apparel and jewelry at three locations.
✚ E5 ✉ 1511 1st Avenue
☎ 206/624–2529
✚ D4 ✉ 215 Broadway E
☎ 206/328–7451
✚ A6 ✉ 4515 University Way NE ☎ 206/632–8886 🚌 71, 72, 73, 43

RUBY MONTANA'S PINTO PONY
The ultimate in kitsch from the 1950s and 1960s including lava lamps, gag gifts, and what's purported to be the largest salt-and-pepper shaker collection on the West Coast.
✚ G6 ✉ 603 2nd Avenue
☎ 206/621–7669

WE HATS
A playful mix of everything from fine fedoras to court jester hats.
✚ G3 ✉ 105 1st Avenue S
☎ 206/623–3409

THEATER

Ticket/Ticket

Ticket sells remaining tickets for music, dance, theater, and comedy venues at half-price on the day of the show. Cash only, at two locations:

➕ F5 ✉ Pike Place Market at the 1st and Pike Information booth 🕐 Every day except Mon, noon–6PM

➕ D4 ✉ Broadway Market, second level, 401 Broadway E at E Harrison 🕐 Tue–Sat, 10–7; Sun noon–6

A CONTEMPORARY THEATER (ACT)

Contemporary plays May–December; the season always closes with *A Christmas Carol*. Downtown.

➕ C2 ✉ 700 Union Street
☎ 206/292–7676

BATHHOUSE THEATER

Intimate 125-seat Parks Department facility at Green Lake, specializing in innovative productions and contemporary classics.

➕ K2 ✉ 7312 W Green Lake Drive N ☎ 206/524–9108
🚌 16

CREPE DE PARIS

Seattle's downtown dinner theater; French cuisine and cabaret. Terrace. Reservations recommended.

➕ F6 ✉ 1333 5h Avenue at Rainier Square
☎ 206/623–4111
🕐 Mon–Sat

THE EMPTY SPACE THEATER

Bold, imaginative theatrical presentations in funky Fremont.

➕ A3 ✉ 3509 Fremont Avenue N ☎ 206/547–7500
🚌 26

FIFTH AVENUE THEATER

This historic, ornate hall hosts new productions of classic musicals and touring Broadway shows.

➕ F6 ✉ 1308 5th Avenue
☎ 206/625–1900

INTIMAN THEATER

Pulitzer Prize-winning regional company that focuses on modern plays and the classics. Season runs May–December.

➕ C2 ✉ 201 Mercer Street, Seattle Center ☎ 206/269–1900 🚌 1, 2, 13

PARAMOUNT THEATER

A lovingly restored 1920s movie palace that stages touring Broadway blockbusters.

➕ E6 ✉ 911 Pine Street
☎ 206/682–1414

SEATTLE REPERTORY THEATER

Seattle's oldest theater company, with two venues, presents updated classics, recent off-Broadway and regional plays and premiers of works by up-and-coming playwrights. October–May

➕ C2 ✉ Bagley Wright Theater, Seattle Center
☎ 206/443–2222 🚌 1, 2, 1

VELVET ELVIS ARTS LOUNGE THEATER

Alternative arts venue in Pioneer Square featuring theater, rock shows, and film.

➕ G3 ✉ 107 Occidental Avenue S ☎ 206/624–8477

CLASSICAL MUSIC, DANCE & OPERA

CLASSICAL MUSIC

FRYE MUSEUM CONCERT SERIES

The Frye Museum presents free Sunday afternoon chamber music concerts at 2PM roughly twice a month.

✚ E4 ✉ 704 Terry Avenue
☎ 206/622–9250 🚌 3, 4

INTERNATIONAL CHAMBER MUSIC SERIES

Renowned chamber music ensembles perform from fall to spring at the University of Washington.

✚ A5 ✉ Meany Theater, University of Washington, 4001 University Way NE
☎ 206/543–4880

OLYMPIC MUSIC FESTIVAL

The Philadelphia String Quartet and other celebrated musicians perform in a turn-of-the-century barn on the Olympic Peninsula near Port Townsend, June–September.
Information available at:

✚ A5 ✉ 4730½ University Way NE ☎ 206/527–8839

SEATTLE CHAMBER MUSIC FESTIVAL

Popular summer series performances, with pre-concert dining on the lawns of the picturesque Lakeside School.

✚ A4 ✉ Lakeside School, 14050 1st Avenue NE
☎ 206/238–8710 🚌 307 to Northgate, then 317

SEATTLE SYMPHONY ORCHESTRA

A wide variety of classical music concerts September–mid-June

in Benaroya Hall.

✚ C3 ✉ 2nd and University
☎ 206/215–4747

DANCE

MEANY HALL'S WORLD DANCE SERIES

This October–May series features good ballet, modern, and ethnic dance; Seattle native Mark Morris is a frequent presence.

✚ A5 ✉ Meany Hall, University of Washington campus
☎ 206/543–4880

ON THE BOARDS/ CENTER FOR CONTEMPORARY PERFORMANCE

Avant-garde presentations that integrate dance, theater, music, and visual media.

✚ C2 ✉ 100 West Roy
☎ 206/325–7902 🚌 15, 18

PACIFIC NORTHWEST BALLET

Renowned company under the direction of former New York City Ballet dancers. The repertory mixes contemporary and classical, including rarely performed Balanchine ballets .

✚ C3 ✉ Phelps Center, Seattle Center ☎ 206/441–9411
🚌 1, 2, 13

OPERA

SEATTLE OPERA

One of the nation's pre-eminent opera companies, with four or five full-scale productions September–May.

✚ C3 ✉ Opera House, Seattle Center ☎ 206/389–7676
🚌 1, 2, 13

Seattle outdoor concert series

In summer, Seattleites enjoy several outdoor concert series including:

• Out-to-Lunch noontime brown bag concerts at various downtown locations.

• Wednesday evening folk and pop concerts at the Woodland Park zoo bandshell.

• Summer Nights at the Pier, a waterfront concert series featuring big-name performers of pop, rock, R&B, and blues. Third week of June through late August.

✚ F5 ✉ Pier 62/63 by the Aquarium ☎ Hotline: 206/281–8111

ROCK, JAZZ & BLUES VENUES

Join the club

Sub Pop Records, the local company that brought you Nirvana, Soundgarden, Alice in Chains, and others, continues to produce recordings of cutting-edge groups on the way up. If you like being among the first to spot a winner, join Sub Pop Singles Club and you'll receive two limited edition 45s records every other month.

✉ Sub Pop Records, Inc. P.O. Box 20645, Seattle 98102 ☎ 800/SUBPOP1 or e-mail: singlesclub@subpop.com

CROCODILE

Hippest local and touring bands play for a tattooed and pierced 20-something crowd at this birthplace of grunge, still co-owned by wife of REM guitarist Peter Buck.
✚ E5 ✉ 2200 2nd Avenue ☎ 206/448–2114

DIMITRIOU'S JAZZ ALLEY

Legendary jazz performers in a pleasant setting. Dinner before ensures a good seat.
✚ D3 ✉ 2033 Sixth Aven ue ☎ 206/441–9729

FENIX/FENIX UNDERGROUND

Live music every Thursday and Saturday, and alternating Wednesdays and Fridays. Rock to reggae to world music.
✚ G6 ✉ 315 2nd Avenue S at Jackson ☎ 206/467–1111

LARRY'S GREENFRONT

Blues, R&B, and burgers in Pioneer Square.
✚ G6 ✉ 209 1st Avenue S ☎ 206/624–7665

NEW ORLEANS CREOLE RESTAURANT

Cajun zydeco and jazz in Pioneer Square.
✚ G6 ✉ 114 1st Avenue S ☎ 206/622–2563

OK HOTEL

Café/bar under the Alaskan viaduct between Washington and Main with music and poetry slams in the lounge.
✚ G6 ✉ 212 Alaskan Way S ☎ 206/621–7903

THE PAMPAS CLUB

Round tables, white linen, understated lighting, a large dance floor, and a stage big enough for large bands. Cabaret-style entertainment—primarily Latin jazz and world music.
✚ D3 ✉ 90 Wall Street ☎ 206/728–1140

THE SHOWBOX

This larger venue does everything from live shows of popular touring and local groups to rock and jazz to DJ dance and theme nights, Thursday to Sunday.
✚ E5 ✉ 1426 First Avenue ☎ 206/628–3151

SIT 'N' SPIN

Seattle sound: do your laundry, play board games, eat black bean chili or foccacia sandwiches, and listen to up-and-coming Seattle rock groups before they hit the Crocodile.
✚ E5 ✉ 2219 4th Avenue ☎ 206/441–9484

TRACTOR TAVERN

This folksy and congenial club is one of the leading supporters of Celtic music. Good acts.
✚ Off map at A1 ✉ 5213 Ballard Avenue NW ☎ 206/789–3599

OTHER VENUES & HANGOUTS

COMEDY UNDERGROUND

National and local comedy acts with audience participation.

✚ G6 ✉ 222 S Main Street ☎ 206/628-0303

ENTROS

Billed as "the only intelligent amusement park in the world". Come for the interactive social games that are debuted here. The on-site World Grille features international fare; games run continuously and can be visited in any order. Best on weekends.

✚ D4 ✉ 823 Yale Avenue North ☎ 206/624-0057 🕐 Closed Sun-Mon

GAMEWORKS

Video arcade features state-of-the-art games. Especially popular with teens and twenty-somethings.

✚ F6 ✉ 1511 7th Avenue ☎ 206/521-0952 or 206/521-9293

GIGGLES

Microbrews on tap, cheap eats, and hit-and-miss comedy. College crowd. University District.

✚ A6 ✉ 5220 Roosevelt Way NE ☎ 206/526-5653

PACIFIC SCIENCE CENTER LASER SHOWS

Laser light shows to rock music Tuesday to Sunday evenings in the domed laser theater. The daily matinees, some with laser animation, are appropriate for families.

✚ D2 ✉ 2nd N at Seattle Center ☎ 206/443-2850

RICHARD HUGO HOUSE

Seattle's welcoming literary arts gathering place on Capitol Hill. Frequent readings and other inventive programming.

✚ D4 ✉ 1634 11th Avenue ☎ 206/322-7030

SHORTY'S

Vintage pinball, video games, Coney Island hotdogs, and nachos in Belltown.

✚ E5 ✉ 2222 2nd Avenue ☎ 206/441-5449 🕐 Mon-Sat 11AM-midnight, Sun 3-10

THEATERSPORTS

Unexpected Productions presents improvisational drama, evenings at the Market Theater.

✚ F5 ✉ 1428 Post Alley at the Pike Street Market ☎ 206/781-9273

TUBS

Rooms with hot tubs for rent by the hour. University District.

✚ A6 ✉ 50th and Roosevelt Way NE ☎ 206/527-8827

Speakeasy Café

One of the world's first Internet cafés, where members walk in and check their e-mail or surf the Web over coffee, beer, pastries, or lunch. Jazz and ambient music in the lounge after 9 Thu-Sat. Also experimental film, poetry reading, and music in the Backroom. Over 21s after 9PM.

✚ D3 ✉ 2304 Second Avenue ☎ 206/728-9770 🕐 Closed Mon; after 9PM, 21 and older only.

BARS, PUBS & TAVERNS

FIRESIDE ROOM
With its overstuffed chairs and fireplace, this spot in the lobby of the stately Sorrento Hotel takes you back to earlier, more genteel times.
✚ F6 ✉ 900 Madison Street ☎ 206/622–6400

FX MCRORY'S STEAK CHOP & OYSTER HOUSE
With a first-rate oyster bar, more than 140 bourbons, and 26 beers on tap, this sparkling brass-and-wood establishment across from the Kingdome attracts both professional athletes and sports fans. Full bar; noisy.
✚ G6 ✉ 419 Occidental Avenue S ☎ 206/623–4800 🕐 Till midnight

HARBOUR PUBLIC HOUSE
Wonderful neighborhood pub just a short walk from the ferry dock, on Bainbridge Island. Good burgers, fish'n'chips, and pasta.
✚ L2 ✉ 231 Parfitt Way SW on Bainbridge ☎ 206/842–0969

HOPSCOTCH
60 single-malt Scotches, 16 microbrews, and good food in a pleasant Capitol Hill setting.
✚ D5 ✉ 332 15th Avenue E ☎ 206/322–4191 🚇 10

KELL'S IRISH RESTAURANT & PUB
The elegance of a Dublin supper room and the warmth of an Irish pub. Irish music. A market favourite.
✚ F5 ✉ 1916 Post Alley ☎ 206/728–1916

THE PIKE PUB & BREWERY
Good food, a microbrew museum, and excellent craft beers.
✚ F5 ✉ 1415 First Avenue (in the Market) ☎ 622–6044 🕐 Daily–midnight

QUEEN CITY GRILL
Belltown's classiest pub. The first-rate kitchen specializes in grilled entrées. Chic, crowded, and noisy.
✚ E5 ✉ 2201 1st Avenue ☎ 206/443–0975

VIRGINIA INN
An institution—with art on the walls, and a posted quotation providing food for thought for an eclectic group of patrons.
✚ E5 ✉ 1937 1st Avenue ☎ 206/728–1937 🕐 Mon–Thu 11AM– midnight; Fri–Sat 11AM–2AM; Sun noon–midnight

VON'S GRAND CITY CAFÉ
The city's best martini "or your money back." Prime rib and fruitwood-smoked turkey stand out in this classic dark wood establishment papered with political cartoons from Seattle papers, quirky memorabilia, photographs, and witty quotes.
✚ E6 ✉ 619 Pine St ☎ 206/621–8667

SPECTATOR SPORTS VENUES

BASEBALL
The Mariners, Seattle's professional baseball team, play in the American Baseball League West.
⊞ F4 ✉ Kingdome Occidental S and S King Street
☎ 206/628–3555

BASKETBALL
The Seattle SuperSonics, the city's oldest professional sports franchise, shoot hoops at home in Key Arena (formerly the Coliseum) Oct–Apr.
⊞ D2 ✉ 1st Avenue N at Seattle Center ☎ 206/283–3865 🚌 1, 2, 13

Seattle's new women's ABL team, the Seattle Reign, play women's basketball in the Mercer Arena, Oct–Feb.
⊞ C3 ✉ 365 Mercer Street, Seattle Center ☎ 206/285–5225 🚌 1, 2, 13

FOOTBALL
Seattle's NFL team, the Seahawks, play ten home games Aug–Dec, in the Kingdome; they're scheduled to move to a new football stadium in 2002.
⊞ F4 ✉ Kingdome Occidental S and S King Street
☎ 206/682–2800 🚌 71, 72, 73, 43, 25

The University of Washington's Huskies play PAC-10 football in fall at the 72,000-seat Husky Stadium
⊞ A5 ✉ Montlake Blvd. NE
☎ 206/543–2200

HOCKEY
The WHL's Seattle Thunderbirds play hockey in Key Arena Sep–Mar.
⊞ D2 ✉ 400 1st Avenue N
☎ 206/448–7825 🚌 1, 2, 13

HORSE-RACING
The city's track is at Emerald Downs in Auburn, south of Seattle. Live thoroughbred racing Thursday through Sunday from the end of March through the end of September as well as special events in summer.
⊞ N3 ✉ 2300 Emerald Downs Drive, Auburn
☎ 206/253/288–7000
🕐 First race weekdays at 5, weekends and holidays at 1

HYDROPLANE RACES
Held every August since 1950 on a 2-mile course south of the Lake Washington floating bridge, as the grande finale to Seattle's Seafair celebration. Hydroplanes, powered by helicopter turbine engines, reach speeds over 150 mph.
⊞ L3 ☎ 206/728–0123 for viewing area tickets

SOCCER
The Seattle Seadogs play CISL's soccer indoors Jun–Sep at Key Arena.
⊞ D2 ✉ 400 1st Avenue N
☎ 206/281–5800 🚌 1, 2, 13

Ticketmaster
Tickets to many of Seattle's sporting events, as well as concerts, are available from this outlet.
☎ 206/628–8888

LUXURY HOTELS

Prices

$ = under $60
$$ = $60–130
$$$ = Over $130

Discounts and promotions

Many of the larger hotels and some smaller ones offer special corporate rates or discounts running about 10 percent for AAA and AARP members. Some establishments accept Entertainment cards, which can reduce prices 50 percent; in addition, those catering to business travelers may have reduced rates while on weekends; in addition, most accommodations lower their rates in the off-season.

ALEXIS HOTEL
Small downtown hotel with tasteful post-modern styling and impeccable service.
✚ F6 ✉ 1007 1st Avenue ☎ 206/ 624–4844 or 800/426–7033

FOUR SEASONS OLYMPIC HOTEL
Seattle's best hotel. Spa, and pool plus the lavish Georgian Room. High tea in Garden Court is lovely.
✚ F6 ✉ 411 University Street ☎ 206/621–1700

HOTEL MONACO
Lively and stylish; personable staff, and fun restaurant—Sazerac. Some rooms have two-person soaking tubs.
✚ F6 ✉ 1101 4th Ave ☎ 206/621–1770, fax: 206/624–0060

HOTEL VINTAGE PARK
This European-style hotel offers good value and attentive service. Fax/internet access, voicemail, and valet parking.
✚ F6 ✉ 1100 5th Avenue at Spring. ☎ 206/624–8000; fax: 206/623–0568

INN AT HARBOR STEPS
Elegant retreat near Seattle Art Museum, Market, and the waterfront. Well-appointed rooms, fireplaces, fitness center, pool, and spa.
✚ F6 ✉ 1221 1st Avenue ☎ Toll-free 888-728–8910

INN AT THE MARKET
This charming 69-room hotel with French provincial decor shares a brick courtyard with several shops and Campagne Restaurant, on the east side of the Pike Place Market.
✚ F5 ✉ 86 Pine Street ☎ 206/443–3600 or 800-446–4484; fax: 206/448–0631

MAYFLOWER PARK
An elegant, intimate hotel in a renovated 1920s building near Westlake Center. Small workout facility. Home of the popular bar/lounge and the romantic Andaluca Restaurant.
✚ E5 ✉ 405 Olive Way ☎ 206/ 623–8700; fax: 206/382–6996

SHERATON SEATTLE HOTEL & TOWERS
This downtown tower with a striking lobby and 840 luxury rooms filled with art by Northwest artists. Health club and Fullers Restaurant; first-rate concierge staff.
✚ E6 ✉ 1400 6th Avenue ☎ 621–9000

WESTIN SEATTLE
Large downtown hotel with an attractive lobby and a fine concierge and bell staff. Fitness center with indoor pool, and the eminent Nikko's Restaurant. In-room modem hook-ups.
✚ E5 ✉ 1900 5th Avenue at Stewart ☎ 800/228–3000; fax: 206/728–2259

MID-RANGE HOTELS

BEST WESTERN EXECUTIVE INN
123 new units near the Seattle Center Restaurant/lounge.
➕ D3 ✉ 200 Taylor N
☎ 206/448-9444

EXECUTIVE INN EXPRESS
Furnished apartment suites near hospitals on south Capitol Hill. Units have kitchens, washer-dryer, telephones with private lines and data ports; fitness center, spa. Complimentary shuttle to downtown.
➕ D4 ✉ 300 10th Avenue
☎ 206/223-9300(collect); fax: 206/233-0241

HAMPTON INN DOWNTOWN
This new motor inn at Seattle Center has an attractive lobby and rooms. Continental breakfast, premium cable TV, 24-hour fitness room. Excellent value.
➕ D3 ✉ 700 5th Avenue North ☎ 206/282-7700 or 800/HAMPTON; fax: 206/282-0899 🚌 3, 4, 6; Monorail to downtown.

HOTEL SEATTLE
Conveniently located downtown hotel. Restaurant/lounge serves breakfast and lunch.
➕ F6 ✉ 315 Seneca
☎ 206/623-5110 and 800/426-2439; fax: 206/623-5110

PACIFIC PLAZA HOTEL
Convenient downtown location; continental breakfast.
➕ F6 ✉ 400 Spring Street
☎ 206/623-3900 or 800/426-1165; fax: 623-2059

PIONEER SQUARE HOTEL
Restored turn-of-the-century hotel in Pioneer Square. Close to the waterfront and the Kingdome.
➕ G6 ✉ 77 Yesler Way
☎ 206/340-1234; fax: 206/467-0707

RAMADA INN
Downtown hotel within walking distance of Westlake Center and Seattle Center. Attractive lobby and on-site restaurant. A good choice if you've got a car.
➕ D3 ✉ 2200 5th Avenue
☎ 206/441-9785 or 800/228-2828

WESTCOAST VANCE HOTEL
Lovingly restored old hotel downtown. The rooms and baths are tiny but well-appointed and spotless.
➕ E6 ✉ 620 Stewart Street
☎ 206/441-4200; fax: 306/441-8612

B&Bs

Gaslight Inn
Lovingly restored turn-of-the-century mansion and annex. Well-appointed rooms, charming courtyard with plantings and a small swimming pool. Ten minutes to downtown.
➕ D5 ✉ 1727 15th Avenue
☎ 206/325-3654 🚌 10, 43

Inn at Queen Anne
Comfortable 67-room inn in an older brick building next to Seattle Center. Complimentary breakfast, kitchenettes, cable TV, voicemail and air conditioning.
➕ C2 ✉ 505 1st Avenue N
☎ 206/282-7357 or 800/952-5043

Salisbury House
Charming, beautifully restored and decorated 1904 home on a residential street on north Capitol Hill. A gem.
➕ C5 ✉ 750 16th Avenue E
☎ 206/328-8682; fax: 206/720-1019

85

BUDGET ACCOMMODATION

HOTELS

COLLEGE INN GUEST HOUSE
The upper floors of this 1904 Tudor building house a pension with 25 rooms, each with a bed, wash basin, writing desk and chair, and shared bathroom. Bountiful continental breakfast. Café and pub downstairs.
A5 4000 University Way NE 206/633–4441

www.speakeasy.org/collegeinn $53.75
Street Parking (inclusive)
Std rm dbl bed
3/10 - 3/12
#030104-0
40th & Univ.

spartan but clean, with bath and TV. Funky.
E5 1926 2nd Avenue 206/448–4851 or 800/421–5508

MV CHALLENGER BUNK & BREAKFAST
Renovated tugboat anchored on Lake Union with eight nautical-motif cabins. In addition, you can rent one of three anchored yachts.
C4 1001 Fairview Avenue N 206/340–1201; fax: 206/621–9208

HOSTELS

GREEN TORTOISE HOSTEL
At the Pike Place Market. Shared and private rooms: linen provided. Shared kitchen, and common room with stereo, TV, and VCR; lockers and laundry facilities.
F5 1525 2nd Avenue 206/340–1222 or toll-free 1–888/424–6783; fax: 206/623–3207 Free bus zone

SEATTLE INTERNATIONAL HOSTEL (AYH)
Bunkrooms for 4–6 people; Ample shared kitchen and common room; library with travel books and other resources. Non-members welcome but AYH members are given priority in busy seasons.
F5 84 Union St (1st-Western) 206/622–5443

YWCA
Good central downtown location. Singles and doubles, some with private baths. Shared kitchen; nearby health center available. Women only.
F6 1118 5th Avenue 206/461–4888; fax 206/461–4860

SEATTLE
travel facts

ARRIVING & DEPARTING

When to go

- July and August are prime months to visit—sunny and clear with usually no more than an inch of rain. Days are long with temperatures in the 70s and 80s; nights can be quite cool. Bring a sweater or light jacket and come prepared to dress in layers.
- November to January are the rainiest months.
- Spring comes early in Seattle, bringing a flurry of bulbs and flowering trees. Despite weather, which is sometimes unsettled—alternating between clouds, showers, and sunshine on any given day—it is a favorite time for many.
- September is often lovely, with temperatures ranging between 70–50°F and rainfall averaging 1.88 inches.

Climate

- Moderate temperatures year-round averaging: Dec–Jan: 46°F; Mar–May: 58°F; Jun–Aug: 73°F; Sep–Nov: 53°F.
- Total annual precipitation averages 34–37 inches (less than New York and Boston). Many days are cloudy or partly cloudy.
- Precipitation comes as rain—generally a light drizzle or intermittent showers. Thunderstorms are rare. Snow is infrequent in Seattle, itself, but the Cascades and Olympic Mountains receive vast quantities; ski areas generally open by late November.

Arriving by air

- Sea-Tac International Airport is 13 miles south of Seattle via I-5
- Travelers Aid on the ticketing level offers free information on getting around, and escorts children, the elderly, and disabled: Mon–Fri 9:30–9:30, Sat–Sun 10–6.
- An airport information desk near baggage claim provides current information on ground transportation. Airport information: (☎ 206/433–5388)
- Bus service to downtown hotels at half-hour intervals, 5AM–11PM via Gray Line Airport Express (☎ (206/626–6088).
- Door-to-door van service to and from airport: SuperShuttle (☎ 206/622–1424 or 1–800/487–RIDE).
- Taxis line up at a stand outside of baggage claim. Fares run about $25–30 without tip.
- City buses to downtown leave from Sea-Tac baggage claim level. Call Metro (☎ 206/553–3000) for schedule information.

Arriving by bus

- Greyhound Bus Lines (✉ 811 Stewart Street) connects Seattle to other cities. Greyhound Information ☎ (800/231–2222.
- Green Tortoise Alternative Travel makes twice weekly runs between Seattle and Los Angeles. Call ☎ 800/867–8647.

Arriving by car

- Visitors arriving by car from the north or south will enter the city via I-5. Downtown exits are: Union Street (for City Center) and James Street (for Pioneer Square).
- Those arriving via I-90 from the east will cross the Lake Washington floating bridge and follow signs to I-5 north for downtown exits.

Arriving by train

- Trains arrive at King Street

Station at 3rd and Jackson between Pioneer Square and the International District.
- For reservations or information, call Amtrak: (☎ 1–800/872–7245)

ESSENTIAL FACTS

Electricity
- 110 volts, 60 cycles AC current.
- Electrical outlets are for flat, two-prong plugs. European appliances require an adaptor.

Etiquette
- Seattle dress is informal; for most places, a jacket and tie are optional.
- Seattle has one of the most successful recycling programs in the country. Many public places provide separate trash bins for paper, aluminum cans, and glass. Littering is not tolerated.
- Seattle is difficult for smokers. Most public places prohibit smoking, and many restaurants that permit smoking provide a special seating area. Outdoor patios and bars are more likely to allow smoking.
- Tipping 15–20 percent is customary in restaurants; 15 percent for taxicabs.

Operating hours
- Banks: Generally Mon–Fri 9:30–5, some open Sat mornings.
- Offices: Normally Mon–Fri 9–5.
- Stores downtown open between 9–10AM and typically close at 5–6PM. with some staying open till 9 on Thursday evenings. Stores in shopping malls generally stay open Mon–Sat till 9PM; Sun till 5 or 6PM.

National Holidays
- New Year's Day (1 Jan)
- Martin Luther King Day (third Mon in Jan)
- President's Day (third Mon in Feb)
- Memorial Day (last Mon in May)
- Independence Day (4 July)
- Labor Day (first Mon in Sept)
- Columbus Day (second Mon in Oct)
- Veterans' Day (11 Nov)
- Thanksgiving (fourth Thu in Nov)
- Christmas Day (25 Dec)

Money matters
- Unit of currency is the U.S. dollar (= 100 cents). Bills come in denominations of $1, $5, $10, $20, $50 and $100; coins are 50¢ (a half-dollar), 25¢ (a quarter), 10¢ (a dime), 5¢ (a nickel), and 1¢ (a penny).
- Money-changing facilities are available at Sea-Tac Airport, every major bank and at Thomas Cook (✉ 9906 3rd Avenue, downtown ☎ 206/623–6203).
- Most major establishments and businesses accept major credit cards like Visa and American Express. Make sure to bring your personal identity number (PIN) in order to use cash machines. Few places accept personal checks; bring travelers' checks.
- Automatic Teller Machines (ATMs) are available at virtually all banks.

Discounts
- Ticket/Ticket: Half-price day-of-show tickets (cash only): theater, concert, dance, comedy, and music available at two locations: Pike Place Market Info Booth (✉ 1st and Pike and Broadway Market, 401 Broadway E on Capitol Hill ☎ 206/324–2744 🕒 Closed Mon).
- If you want to visit Seattle's most popular tourist attractions, get a CityPass ticket book—it will

reduce admissions' prices by 50 percent to Woodland Park Zoo, Space Needle, Pacific Science Center, Seattle Aquarium, and Museum of Flight. Passbooks can be purchased at any of the six attractions and are valid for seven days.

- Student travelers are advised to bring a current student ID to obtain discounted admissions.

Places of worship

Check the Yellow Pages of the phone book for complete listing. Prominent houses of worship include:

- Catholic: St. James Cathedral (☒ 9th and Marion ☎ 206/622–3559)
- Congregational: Plymouth Congregational Church (☒ 6th and University ☎ 206/622–4865)
- Episcopal: St Marks Episcopal Cathedral (☒ 1245 10th Avenue E (Capitol Hill) ☎ 206/323–0300)
- Greek Orthodox: St Demetrios Greek Orthodox Church (☒ 2100 Boyer E ☎ 206/325–4347)
- Lutheran: Gethsemane Lutheran Church (☒ 9th & Stewart ☎ 206/682–3620)
- Methodist: First United Methodist (☒ 811 5th Avenue ☎ 206/622–7278)
- Mosque: Islamic (Idriss) Mosque (☒ 1420 NE Northgate Way ☎ 206/363–3013)
- Synagogues: Temple De Hirsch Sinai (☒ 1511 E Pike Street ☎ 206/323–8486; 24 hour info line- 323–TDHS)

Public Restrooms

- Hotels, public buildings, and shopping complexes like Rainier Square are reliable bets for clean restrooms.
- Public restrooms are located in Pike Place Market (base of the ramp in the Main Arcade) and in the Convention Center.

Ticket Outlets

- Ticketmaster (☒ Westlake Center Mall (1601 5th Avenue, suite 400) ☎ 206/628–0888 ☒ Tower Records, 500 Mercer Street ☒ Kingdome, 201 S King Street)
- Ticket/Ticket for same-day discounts (see Discounts).

Time differences

- Seattle is on Pacific Standard Time, three hours behind Eastern Standard Time in New York, eight hours behind the U.K.

Weights and Measures

- Metric equivalents for U.S. weights and measures are:
- Weights: 1 ounce (oz) = 28 grams; 1 pound (lb) = 0.45 kilogram; 1 quart (qt) = 0.9 liter.
- Measurements: 1 inch (") = 2.5 centimeters; 1 foot (') =0.3 meter; 1 yard (yd) = 0.9 meter and 1 mile = 1.6 kilometers.

Visitor Information

- Seattle-King County Convention and Visitors Bureau (☒ level 1, Galleria/800 Convention Place in the Convention Center (8th and Pike) ☎ 206/461–5840 ◷ Mon–Fri 8:30–5).
- Westlake Information Center (☒ 3rd floor of Westlake Center ☎ 206/467–1600); additional centers during summertime at: across from carousel 8 in baggage claim area at Seatacairport, Seattle Center at base of monorail ramp, and Pioneer Square at Occidental and S Main.
- Seattle Center Info (☎ 206/684–7200); recorded events information (☎ 206/684–7165)
- Seattle Public Library offers a Quick Information number (☎ 206/386–INFO)
- National Park Service, Pacific Northwest Region (☒ 915 2nd

Avenue, #442; ☎ 206/22–7450 🕓 Mon–Fri 8–4:30).

- Student travellers are advised to bring a current student ID for discounted admissions.
- Travellers with disabilities: 24 hour telephone operator service for TTY (Telecommunications Device for the Deaf) by dialing ☎ 1–800/855–1155.

Consulates

- British ✉ First Interstate Center, 999 3rd Avenue, 8th floor ☎ 206/622–9255
- Canadian ✉ 412 Plaza 600, 6th Avenue & Stewart Street ☎ 206/443–1372
- French ✉ 801 2nd Avenue, suite 1500 ☎ 206/624–7855
- German ✉ 600 University Street, suite 2500 ☎ 206/682–4312
- Japanese ✉ 601 Union Street, suite 500 ☎ 206/682–9107
- Mexican ✉ 2132 Third Avenue ☎ 206/448–3526
- New Zealand ✉ PO Box 51059 ☎ 206/525–0271

PUBLIC TRANSPORT

Bicycle

- Seattle is extremely bicycle-friendly. The city has a number of bicycle routes or trails and *Bicycling* magazine has called Seattle the best North American city for bicycling (despite its steep hills.) For Bicycle Rentals, see Active Pursuits, (➤ 56–57.)

Metro Buses

- At press time Seattle's Bus schedules are undergoing major changes. Before a journey please telephone the information line below or contact a tourist office: Metro 24-hour Rider Information at ☎ 206/553–3000 or 800/542–7876.
- Timetables available at Westlake Station, on buses and at more

than 500 locations around the city.
- Metro has a Ride Free Area downtown bordered by Battery Street, Jackson Street, Alaskan Way, 6th Avenue, and I-5. Hours are 6AM–7PM.
- The Metro tunnels under Pine Street and 3rd Avenue with five downtown stations: Convention Place, Westlake, University Street, Pioneer Square, and the International District. All tunnel routes stop at each station. Sundays and evenings after hours when the tunnel is closed, tunnel buses run above ground along 3rd Avenue.
- Seattle bus drivers are not required to call out the stops. If you're unsure where to get off, ask your driver to alert you.

Monorail

- The 1.2-mile ride between downtown Westlake Center (✉ 400 Pine Street) and Seattle Center takes only 90 seconds. Trains run every 15 minutes, 9AM–11PM.

Taxis

- Seattle taxis are expensive: the flag-drop charge is $1.80 and it's $1.80 for each additional mile. Pick one up in front of your hotel or phone for a radio-dispatched cab.
- Major companies with 24-hour dispatch service include Yellow Cab, with the largest fleet (☎ 206/62–6500); FarWest (☎ 206/622–1717 or 1–800/USA–TAXI); or Graytop Cab (☎ 206/282–8222)

Washington State Ferries

- Jumbo ferries from Seattle's downtown terminal to Bainbridge Island and Bremerton (on the Kitsap Peninsula) depart regularly from Colman Dock at pier 52 and accommodate both walk-on passengers and automobiles.

91

- Most ferry routes are very busy during weekday commute periods and on sunny weekends. Expect waits of two hours or more for automobiles in summer and on holiday weekends.
- Schedules change seasonally; phone ☎ 206/464–6400 for schedule and route information.
- Additional ferry routes departing from the Seattle environs serve the Kitsap Peninsula, Vashon Island, Whidbey Island, Port Townsend (Olympic Peninsula), the San Juan Islands, and Victoria, British Columbia.
- Credit cards not accepted.
- Passengers to Canada need passports or other proof of citizenship.

Waterfront Streetcar

- A vintage 1927 trolley runs along the waterfront on Alaskan Way from pier 70 at Broad Street to 5th and Jackson in the International District with intermediate stops at Vine, Bell, Pike, University, Madison, Washington Streets, and at Occidental Park in Pioneer Square.
- When you board, pay your fare and ask for a transfer, which is good for 90 minutes of sightseeing before reboarding. Total ride, end to end, takes 20 minutes. Service every 20 minutes to half an hour, Mon–Fri 7–6; Sat–Sun 9:30–6 with extended summer hours.

Community Transit Buses

- Bus service to points outside the city. (☎ 1–800/562–1375).

MEDIA & COMMUNICATIONS

Mail

- For up-to-date information on postal charges call ☎ 1–800/562–1375

- Minimum charges for a postcard or airmail letter (weighing up to ½ ounce) are currently 46¢ (to Canada), 40¢ (to Mexico), and 60¢ elsewhere.
- Post offices: The main downtown post office is on the corner of Union and 3rd Avenue. Hours are Mon–Fri 8–5:30. Closed Sat–Sun. Branch offices are located in most neighborhoods; most are open Mon–Fri, between 7–9AM with closing times at 5 or 6PM. Some, including the Capitol Hill station, have Saturday hours, 9–1 PM. (✉ 101 Broadway E ☎ 206/324–2588).
- You can buy books of stamps without a markup at many supermarket check-out counters,

Telephones

- Seattle's area code (206) includes Bainbridge Island and Vashon Island. Dialing from one city location to another does not require an area code.
- To make a local call from a pay phone, listen for a dial tone before depositing money, then deposit coins; wait for new dial tone and dial the number.
- Local calls from a pay phone cost 35¢.
- Phonecards for long-distance calls are readily available at convenience stores and elsewhere.
- To pay cash for long-distance calls, follow the same initial procedure as for local calls, and a recorded operator message will tell you how much additional money to deposit for the first three minutes; then deposit additional coins and dial.
- The area running east of Lake Washington from Everett to Maple Valley and east to Snoqualmie pass uses area code (425). The (253) area code runs south from Renton to the Pierce-

Thurston county line. Other calls within western Washington—for example to Port Townsend or the San Juan Islands—require dialing a (360) area code.

- Directory assistance is a toll call. For information, dial 1plus the area code plus the number plus the 555–1212

Newspapers and magazines

- Seattle has two daily papers: an evening paper, *The Seattle Times* (☎ 206/464–2111) and the morning *Seattle Post-Intelligencer* (☎ 206/44–8000). On Fridays *The Times* offers a special arts and entertainment section.
- Weeklies with extensive entertainment listings include the alternative *Stranger* and *The Weekly*. Both are free.
- Seattle's Concierge Association publishes its own magazine, *Where*, with current listings; it's available at Visitor Information booths.
- International newspapers are sold at *Read All About It* (✉ 93 Pike Street at the Pike Place Market ☎ 206/624–0140) and *Bulldog News* (✉ 401 Broadway E ☎ 206/322–NEWS and 4208 University Way NE ☎ 206/632–NEWS).

Radio and Television:

- Seattle's two National Public Radio stations (NPR) are KUOW at 94.9 FM (all-talk radio with news from the BBC) and KPLU, an award-winning jazz station at 88.5 FM.
- KING-FM (98.1) plays classical music.
- Seattle's six local television channels are: KOMO 4 (ABC); KING 5 (NBC); 7 (CBS); KCTS/9 (PBS); KSTW 11 (independent); and 13 (Fox).

EMERGENCIES

Emergency phone numbers

- Police, ambulance, or fire: ☎ 911
- The Red Cross Language Bank provides free, on-call interpretive assistance in emergency or crisis situations.

Safety/Crime

- Seattle has its share of crime; exercise caution and at night avoid the areas around 1st to 2nd and Pike, the edges of Pioneer Square, and the area between 2nd and 4th from Cherry to Yesler.
- Seattle police are well-known for ticketing jaywalkers.

Lost Property

- Airport lost and found (☎ 206/433–5312).
- King Street Station lost and found (☎ 206/382–4128).
- Metro bus lost and found (☎ 206/553–3090).

Medical treatment

- Virginia Mason Fourth Avenue Clinic operates a walk-in downtown medical clinic (✉ 1221 4th Avenue, downtown 888/862-2737 ◎ Mon–Fri 7–5; Sat 10–1).
- Chec Medical Centers operate several drop-in clinics; closest to downtown is clinic at Denny and Fairview (☎ 206/682-7418).
- Doctor's, Inc. (☎ 206/622-9933) can help find a doctor 24 hours a day.
- Dentist Referral Service (☎ 206/443-7607).
- For prescription medicine, bring a note or an RX from your doctor.
- Downtown pharmacies include Peterson's Pharmacy (✉ 1629 Sixth Avenue ☎ 206/622–5860) or Pacific Drugs (✉ 822 First Avenue ☎ 206/624–1454)

INDEX

CityPack
Seattle

While every care has been taken to ensure the accuracy of the information in this guide, time brings change, and consequently the publisher cannot accept responsibility for errors that may occur. Prudent travelers will therefore want to call ahead to verify prices and other "perishable" information.

Published in the United States by Fodor's Travel Publications, Inc.
Published in the United Kingdom by AA Publishing

Fodor's is a registered trademark of Fodor's Travel Publications, Inc.

ISBN 0-679-00255-3
First Edition

FODOR'S CITYPACK SEATTLE

AUTHOR *Suzanne Tedesko*   CARTOGRAPHY *The Automobile Association*
COPY EDITOR *John Mapps*   *RV Reise- und Verkehrsverlag*
INDEXER *Marie Lorimer*
VERIFIER *Caroline Alder*

Acknowledgments
The Automobile Association would like to thank the following photographers, libraries and associations for their assistance in the preparation of this book:
The Burke Museum of Natural History and Culture 13b; The Boeing Company 48a, 48b; Fifth Avenue Theatre 54 (Dick Busher); Frank O. Gehry & Associates Inc. 31a (Joshua White); Museum of Flight 43a, 43b; Rex Features Ltd 31b; Spectrum Colour Library 21; University of Washington 5a, 44a; Woodland Park Zoo 28b (Renee De Martin).

All remaining pictures were taken by James Tims and are held in the Association's own library (AA Photo Library) with the exception of the following page: Chris Coe 20.

The author would like to thank Jalyn Tani and Jerry Waugh for their invaluable assistance.

Cover photographs
Main picture:James Timms
Inset:James Timms

Special sales
Fodor's Travel Publications are available at special discounts for bulk purchases (100 copies or more) for sales promotions or premiums. Special editions, including personalized covers, excerpts of existing guides, and corporate imprints, can be created in large quantities for special needs. For more information contact your local bookseller or wrtie to Special Marketing, Fodor's Travel Publications, 201 East 50th St., New York NY 10022. Inquiries from Canada should be directed to your local Canadian bookseller or sent to Random House of Canada, Ltd., Marketing Department, 2775 Matheson Bvld. East, Mississanga, Ontario L4W 4P7.

Color separation by Daylight Colour Art Pte Ltd, Singapore
Manufactured by Dai Nippon Printing Co. (Hong Kong) Ltd
10 9 8 7 6 5 4 3 2 1

Titles in the Citypack series
- Amsterdam ● Atlanta ● Beijing ● Berlin ● Boston ● Brussels & Bruges ●
- Chicago ● Dublin● Florence ● Hong Kong ● London ● Los Angeles ●
- Madrid ● Miami ● Montréal ● Moscow ● New York ● Paris ● Prague ●
- Rome ● San Francisco ● Seattle ● Shanghai ● Sydney ● Tokyo ● Toronto ●
- Venice ● Vienna ● Washington DC ●